S0-AVA-053

NUMBERS
THEIR MEANING AND MAGIC

NUMBERS

Their Meaning and Magic

ISIDORE KOZMINSKY

LATE FELLOW OF THE ROYAL HISTORICAL SOCIETY
LATE FELLOW OF THE ROYAL NUMISMATIC SOCIETY
ASSOCIATE OF THE BRITISH ARCHAEOLOGICAL SOCIETY (LONDON)
ETC. ETC.

SAMUEL WEISER INC.

New York

First Published 1912
First American Paperback Edition 1972
Reprinted 1977

ISBN 0-87728-184-X

Samuel Weiser, Inc.
734 Broadway
New York, N.Y. 10003

Printed in the USA by
Noble Offset Printers, Inc.
New York

CONTENTS

NUMBERS

THEIR MEANING AND MAGIC

INTRODUCTION

IT is now seven years since the fourth edition of *Numbers* was published. The editions ran through a few thousand copies, proving that a large section of the public were ready and eager for knowledge on so obscure a subject. Many new points then introduced were accepted by occult and religious writers, and were reprinted in various books and magazines. Too little consideration is given as a rule to the naming of children, the naming of ships, the naming of cities, etc. " What's in a name ? " is the question usually asked by the person who has never given a modicum of thought to the subject. I am endeavouring to show how much there really *is* in a name, and I believe that the evidence produced in this book is at least sufficient to prove this. It seems quite enough in most families, when a child is about to be named, to call it after a grandfather or some other relative near or far, regardless as to its fitness in the case. Hence, knowingly or unknowingly, a child is handicapped

from the cradle. The true thinker is very careful
as to his attitude on obscure subjects, and it is not
right that materialism should so blind a man to the
fact that science is extensive and does not entirely
confine itself to external things. Man can rise
above mere clay, and by the use of his Divine faculties
seek to draw himself nearer to the Ideal, and to
enjoy a little the glories he has lost. Too many
examples of bad naming confront us every day.
True it is that a child may be unfortunate from the
cradle, but that is no argument against the power
of a good name. The disaster to the *Titanic* should
warn shipbuilders and owners not only to see that
their ships are well named, but also to insist on the
keel being laid on a strong and favourable day.
No attention should be paid to the scoffing materialistic and external reasoning mind in a matter of
this kind. The safety of the public is the first
consideration—the first and final. New cities
should also be considered in the same way. London
is a powerful name. It is 31 strong in itself, and
when properly reduced signifies " The Emperor,"
" The Stone Cube," etc. In the simple words of
our language, in common with the most complex,
the student will find additional interest. For
example, the word LOVE equals 21, "The Universe";
HATE equals 15, " The Devil " ; JUSTICE equals 22,
" The Blind Fool " ; whilst SWORD also equals 22.
It may be as well to reflect on human justice of
to-day before we attempt to judge one another in
this world.

Before concluding this brief introduction, I think
it necessary to impress on the student the importance

of a close and proper study of the Bible, one of the greatest gifts of the ancient masters to this world. That the great Book has lost largely by translation and retranslation is beyond the shadow of a doubt ; and many fine passages are altogether inaccurate and misleading. For example, in Job xxxviii. ver. 31, "HATHEQESHER MODENUTH KIMAH AO MOSHECOTH KESIL TIPETECH" is freely rendered into English thus : "Canst thou bind the sweet influence of the Pleiades or loosen the bands of Orion ? " when it should be : "Canst thou bind the tremblings of heat or loose the seals of coldness ? " There is nothing here about either the Pleiades or Orion, and it is evident that the old translators lacked sufficient scientific knowledge when endeavouring to render the passage into English. No man of knowledge in the ancient world would have written of the "sweet influence of the Pleiades." Situated in 27 degrees of Taurus, it is known to-day amongst students of astrology as a dangerous point which has a distinctly adverse influence on the eyes, especially when the sun, moon, or planets are afflicted therein. To go further into the matter I should be compelled to bring the great science of astrology to my aid, and this, of course, I cannot do at present. I only quote the verse as evidence of bad translation, and the translations we have are full of such examples. With the aid of modern scientific knowledge we know just what is meant by the binding of heat tremblings and the freeing of cold, which ancient scholars knew some ages past. The true occult scholar cannot be included in the ranks of Bible critics ; the Book to him is a library of excellence and a treasury of true knowledge.   The translators of the Bible have done much harm in attempting too many liberties with the text.   One day, perhaps, sufficient inducement will be offered to a scholar to produce a perfected edition of the Holy Book with a view to the correct understanding of it by those who esteem " Wisdom better than strength, better than weapons of war."

ISIDORE KOZMINSKY.

210 CLARENDON STREET, EAST MELBOURNE,
VICTORIA, AUSTRALIA.

CHAPTER I

"And Proclus says, number hath always a being: yet there is one in voice—another in proportion of them—another in the soul and reason, and another in Divine things. But Themistius, Boëtius, and Averrois—the Babylonian—together with Plato, do so extol numbers, that they think no man can be a true philosopher without them. By them there is a way made for the searching out and understanding of all things knowable; by them the next access to natural prophesying is had,—and the Abbot Joachim proceeded no other way in his prophecies but by formal numbers. There lies wonderful efficacy and virtue in numbers as well to good as to bad. Simple numbers signify divine things; numbers of ten celestial; numbers of a hundred terrestrial; numbers of a thousand those things that shall be in a future age. Besides, seeing the parts of the mind are according to an arithmetical mediocrity, by reason of the identity, or equality of excess, coupled together; but the body, whose parts differ in their greatness is, according to a geometrical mediocrity, compounded; but an animal consists of both, viz. soul and body, according to that mediocrity which is suitable to harmony. Hence it is that *numbers* work very much upon the *soul*, *figures* upon the *body*, and *harmony* upon the *whole animal*."—FRANCIS BARRETT, F.R.S. 1801.

FOREWORD

In treating in an entirely elementary fashion a subject so vast as that of *numbers*, it is in my opinion necessary that the wisdom of Quaballistical lore should be presented in an easy and intelligible form. Holding this as a first consideration, I am prevented from occupying the pages at my disposal with any history or description of the collected and powerful writings of the ancient sages who

have in some instances departed from this earth
without leaving the merest trace of their identity.
We accept their wisdom in silent thankfulness, and
endeavour with the knowledge at our disposal to
understand it.

THE SYMBOLS AND MEANINGS OF THE NUMBERS

THE NUMBER ONE

One is the Supreme Commander and the Mighty
Unknowable God of the Universe who can be *felt*
by those who have entered into the spiritual light,
but can never be explained.   It is the Divine Mind,
the Fire which appeared to Moses burning, yet not
consuming, the bush ; He who " in the beginning "
had by desire created the Universe, and whose
Power was simply obeyed by the rulers of the
grosser substances.   One is then the Number of
Creation, for out of One come all others, therefore
the " Lord Thy God is One God."

In the *Sepher Yetzirah* the 1st Path of Wisdom
is the Supreme Crown and the Hidden Intelligence, the Light, the Glory of the Primal
Essence.

In the Highest Sphere 1 is the Supreme Being from
    whom all virtues and powers flow.

In the Sphere of Intellect 1 is the Soul of the World
    and the First Man.

In the Heavenly Sphere 1 is the Star King the
    Sun, the Life-Giver.

In the Elemental Sphere 1 is the Stone of the
    Philosophers and the primary instrument.

In the Lower Sphere 1 is the Heart—the principle of life and death.

In the Infernal Sphere 1 is Lucifer the Prince of Darkness, and the Rebellious Angels.

The Occult Symbols of the number 1 are—

The Juggler; The Man Adam; Osiris; Apollo.

The Juggler is presented as a beautiful youth with curling hair and with a smile of hope on his face. In one hand he holds a wand with which he points upwards to call the World to the contemplation of the majesty of God; his other hand is lowered, and with it he points downwards to call the World to the contemplation of the mystery of Man, illustrated by the symbols, in the Tarot, of the Cup, the Sword, the Wand, and the Pentacles.

The Hebrew equivalent of the number 1 is the letter Aleph.

It is the Father of Numbers, and is a number of harmony, initiation, activity, self-mastery, subjugation of the lesser forces, mental power, and austerity.

One is always written a fortunate number by all ancient and modern masters. John Heydon, in his *Holy Guide*, holds it as a most prosperous number; and Eliphas Levi, the French master of the Quaballah, knows it as "the intelligible object," "the primative substance."

The Vibrations are Solar.

THE NUMBER TWO

Two is the number of Intellect and the fountainhead of Mental conception. In the 2nd chapter of Genesis the Spirit of God moves amongst the darkness that was on the face of the deep ; the heaven and earth had been created, and the most material modern philosophy agrees with the book of Genesis regarding the formless earth which the Spirit of God shaped according to Divine Idea. Two is then the number of the moulding of gross substance in response to the intellect of the Grand Architect of the Universe. And God said : " It is not good that the man should be alone."

In the *Sepher Yetzirah* the 2nd Path of Wisdom is the Crown of Creation and the Light of Manifesting Intelligence.

In the Highest Sphere 2 are the 2 letters of the names of God, *Yod Hi* and *Aleph Lamed.*

In the Sphere of Intellect 2 are the Angel and the Soul.

In the Heavenly Sphere 2 indicates the 2 great Lights—the Sun and the Moon.

In the Elemental Sphere 2 indicates the 2 elements of life production—Water and Earth.

In the Lower Sphere 2 indicates the great working organs of the soul—the Heart and the Brain.

In the Infernal Sphere 2 indicates the 2 Infernal Chiefs.

Two years was the least term required for the silence of the initiates of Pythagoras. This silence was in some instances to be kept for a longer term, but it was never to be less. During this period they studied but did not express either the opinions of their masters or their own.

The Occult Symbols of the number 2 are—

The Door of the Holy Temple ; the High Priestess ; Eve ; Isis—Juno pointing with one hand to earth, another to heaven. (This latter symbol is of more recent origin.)

The Hebrew equivalent of the number 2 is the letter Beth.

It is the Mother of Numbers and of marriage. It has been termed the middle number, becoming good or bad by combination. St Hierom accounts it an evil number, and it is generally held to be a number of trouble, death, enmity, contention, and unhappiness. Its virtue is the understanding of the workings of occult knowledge. It seems in the majority of cases an evil affixture to the names of earth kings, as instance the following :—

Demetrius II. assassinated.
Anastasius II.   ,,
Charles II. (the Bald) of France, poisoned.
Edmund II. (Ironside), England, murdered.
William II., England, killed.
Henry II.,   ,,   died of grief.
Boleslaus II. (Poland), dethroned.
Almansur, Caliph of Almohades, died in obscurity.
Edward II., England, murdered.
Richard II.,   ,,   murdered.
Albert II., Austria, " the uncrowned Emperor."
Henry II., France, killed in a tournament.
George II., England, died suddenly.

The world's history can be consulted for more examples. The name of a king or ruler may be fortunate in itself, and then the affixture will not bear the same interpretation. Eusebius writes that Pythagoras spoke of Unity as like to God and a good intellect, but of Duality as like to a devil and

an evil intellect, " wherefore the Pythagoreans say
that 2 is not a number, but a certain confusion
of unities." Plutarch says that the disciples of
Pythagoras called 2 the number of strife and
boldness.   Barrett notes—

Two tables of the law.
Two cherubim looking to the propitiatory in
Moses.
Two first people.
Two spirits, good and bad.
Two equinoctials.
Two poles.
Two animals of a kind sent into the ark, etc.

The Vibrations are Lunar.

THE NUMBER THREE

Three is the Light—a holy number.   In the 3rd
verse of the first chapter of Genesis God said, " *Let
there be light* "; then streamed forth the shafts of
light impregnating the intense darkness like to the
spirit entering matter.

Three, then, is the number of the result of the
moulding of substances—the product of union and
the number of perfection.

In the Sepher Yetzirah the 3rd Path of Wisdom
is the Holy Intelligence, and Original Wisdom.

In the Highest Sphere 3 are the Divine principles
and the 3-lettered name.

In the Sphere of Intellect 3 signifies the 3 degrees
of the Blessed and the 3 hierarchies of Angels.

In the Heavenly Sphere 3 indicates the Planetary
Lords of the triplicities.

In the Elemental Sphere 3 indicates the **3** elemental degrees.

In the Lower Sphere 3 signifies the head, the breast, and the region of the Solar Plexus.

In the Infernal Sphere 3 indicates the 3 degrees of the damned, the 3 infernal Judges, and the 3 infernal Furies.

The trinity prevails in ancient and modern religions. The triangle has 3 points ; with the point upwards it signifies Fire and the Heavenly Powers ; with the point downwards it signifies water and the Hosts below. Hence it is used in mystical rites, and esoteric and exoteric Freemasonry. The triangle with point upwards is the type of Mahadeva or Siva—the personification of Fire in Indian rites ; and with the point downwards is the type of Vishnu —the personification of Water. Old astrology regards the 3rd day after new moon as the first fortunate day of the month.

The Occult Symbols of the number 3 are—

The Empress ; the Virgin Diana ; Isis Urania ; Venus Urania ; Horus.

The Empress is pictured as an enthroned and crowned Angel holding in her hand the orb of the world.

The Hebrew equivalent of the number **3** is Ghimel.

It is the number of the highest wisdom and worth, of harmony and action, perfect love, tenderness, and soul force. It represents plenty, fruitfulness, and exertion. The following remarks concerning the number I take from Knicker-bocker :—

" When the world was created, we find land,
water, and sky, and sun, moon, and stars.   Noah
has 3 sons.   There were 3 Patriarchs.   St
Paul speaks of Faith, Hope, and Charity, these
three.   There is also the Holy Trinity.   In
mythology, there are 3 graces—Cerberus, with
3 heads ; Neptune, holding his 3-toothed staff ;
the oracle of Delphi cherished with veneration
the tripod.   In nature we have male, female,
and offspring ; morning, noon, and night.   Trees
group their leaves in threes.   The majority of
mankind die at 30.   What could be done in
mathematics without the aid of the triangle ?
Witness the power of the wedge, and in logic 3
premisses are indispensable.   It is a common phrase
that ' three is a lucky number.' "

The late Prince Bismarck held to this number as
" lucky."   He served 3 emperors, fought in 3
wars, signed 3 peace treaties, arranged the
meeting of the 3 emperors, and formed the
Triple Alliance.   His family arms are the trefoil
leaves, and the 3 oak leaves, with the motto
" IN TRINITATE ROBUR."   He had 3 children,
3 estates, and controlled 3 political parties—
the Conservatives, the Liberals, and the Ultra-
montanes.

In a work entitled *Mediæval Myths*, published
in February 1869, the following interesting note,
kindly sent to me by Mr R. H. Oldershan,
is given :—

" There is said to be a tradition of Norman-
Monkish origin that the number 3 is stamped on
the Royal line of England so that there shall not

be *more* than 3 princes in succession without a revolution—

William I., William II., Henry I. ; then follows the revolution of Stephen.

Henry II., Richard I., John ; invasion of Louis, Dauphin of France, who claimed the throne.

Henry III., Edward I., Edward II., who was dethroned and put to death.

Edward III., Richard II., who was dethroned.

Henry IV., Henry V., Henry VI. ; the crown passed to the Duke of York.

Edward IV., Edward V., Richard III. ; the crown claimed and won by Henry Tudor.

Henry VII., Henry VIII., Edward VI. ; usurpation of Lady Jane Grey.

Mary I., Elizabeth ; the crown passed to the House of Stuart.

James I., Charles I. ; revolution.

Charles II., James II. ; invasion of William of Orange.

William of Orange and Mary II., Anne ; arrival of the House of Brunswick.

George I., George II., George III. The law proves a little faulty here, but there was a crisis in the reign of George IV."

The Vibrations of number 3 are Jupiterian.

THE NUMBER FOUR

This is the number of completion and the manifestation of Light. In the 4th verse of the first chapter of Genesis God divides the Light from the Darkness. It is a number of understanding and order, and the key which will open many of the magical doors closed to ordinary man. "Men of the highest order show themselves in thought like brilliant rays of light," says the "Magicon." They correspond to the number 4. It is the sacred number of the Pythagoreans, and is known by them as the straight line. It was over this number that they took their most sacred oaths.

In the *Sepher Yetzirah* the 4th Path is the grand Crown and the Path from which flow all the powers of Spirit and the Divine essences.

In the Highest Sphere 4 is the 4 letters of the name of God—Yod, Hi, Vau, Hi.

In the Sphere of Intellect 4 is the 4 Angels of the World (Michael, Raphael, Gabriel, Uriel) ; the 4 Rulers of the Elements (Seraph, Cherub, Tharsis, Ariel).

In the Heavenly Sphere 4 is the 4 triplicities of the signs of the Zodiac and the stars and planets in relation to the elements. These are given as Mars and the Sun ; Jupiter and Venus ; Saturn and Mercury ; the fixed stars and the Moon. This grouping is not always accepted. Another is Sun and Saturn ; Jupiter and Venus ; Mercury and Mars ; Moon and the fixed stars.

In the Elemental Sphere 4 is the 4 elements ; the 4 seasons ; the 4 winds ; the 4 divisions of life (Animal, Plant, Metal, Stone) ; the 4 qualities (Heat, Moisture, Cold, Dryness).

In the Lower Sphere 4 is the 4 elements of man (Mind, Spirit, Soul, Body) ; the 4 powers of the soul (Intellect, Reason, Phantasy, Sense) ; the 4 virtues (Justice, Temperance, Prudence, Fortitude) ; the 4 bodily elements (Spirit,

Flesh, Humours, Bones); the 4 humours (Choler, Blood, Phlegm, Melancholy).

In the Infernal Sphere 4 represents the 4 infernal princes (Samael, Azazel, Azael, Mahazael).

In astrology the square is evil possibly because it is symbolic of the pressure of matter, in the same way as the cross of 4 points symbolises the pain of matter. The worshippers of Vishnu account a swastica cross with the small limbs pointing to the right fortunate. The fortunate swastica of the old Jaina kings had the small limbs pointing to the left. A swastica with small curved top limbs is not considered a fortunate emblem ; it is too like the scythe of Death.

The Occult Symbols of the number 4 are—

The Emperor; the Cubic Stone ; the Key-bearer, the Door of the East ; the 4 Cherubim in 4 Wheels ; the 4 Sea Horses of Neptune's Chariot.

The Emperor is pictured seated on a throne with the orb surmounted by a cross in his left hand and a trident sceptre in his right. He is in complete armour, with the signs of the Sun and Moon on his breast. He is bearded, and his expression is strong, yet kindly.

" The Hebrews received the chiefest name of God written with 4 letters," writes Francis Barrett. " Also the Egyptians, Arabians, Persians, Magicians, Mohammedans, Grecians, Tuscans, and Latins write the name of God with four letters, thus—

THET ; ALLA ; SIRE ; ORSI ;
ABDI ; Θεὸς ; ESAR ; DEUS."

In English we have LORD ; in French DIEU ; and in German GOTT.

Man receives from the world of Asiah the Nephesch or physical appetites.

Man receives from the world of Jezirah the Ruach or passions.

Man receives from the world of Briah the Neshamah or reason.

Man receives from the world of Aziluth Chaiah or spiritual life.

According to Quaballistical teaching all the race of man sinned in their parent Adam, for all are contained in him. Thus the children of Adam were condemned to clothe themselves in material prisons or bodies. From these bodies were they to reach again the lost Paradise. When an earth life was passed the child of earth could proceed from Asiah to Jezirah, from Jezirah to Briah, but he could not, unless purified from earth grossness, enter the sunlit world of the angels—Aziluth—and had therefore to re-enter the earth again to begin his penance anew. Thus the philosophy of Reincarnation is quite in harmony with Egyptian, Greek, and Indian philosophy, and the philosophy of other nations regarding it.

Four is the number of endurance and immortality, discovery and accomplishment, firmness of purpose, realisation of hopes, rule, power, will.

The Hebrew equivalent of the number 4 is Daleth.

The Vibrations are Solar, and it is always accounted a fortunate number.

THE NUMBER FIVE

This is a peculiar and magical number, and was used by the Greeks and Romans as an amulet to protect the wearer from evil spirits. It is usually a number of confusion and quarrel, for it is a very intense vibration, and only the one understanding its import can become a magician. It represents irritation and the moulding of the mortal body to the discipline of the spiritual.

In the *Sepher Yetzirah* the 5th Path is Fundamental Intelligence.

In the Highest Sphere 5 is indicative of the 5 letters in the name of God.

In the Sphere of Intellect 5 are the Superior Spirits, the Intelligences; the Angels; the Souls of Heavenly Bodies; the Souls of the Blessed.

In the Heavenly Sphere 5 represents the 5 planets (Saturn, Jupiter, Mars, Venus, Mercury).

In the Elemental Sphere 5 represents Water, Air, Fire, Earth, and another element to be discovered.

In the Lower Sphere 5 represents the 5 senses.

In the Infernal Sphere 5 represents the 5 torments.

The Pentacle or 5-pointed Star was always regarded as possessing power as a talisman of protection and health; and it is said that Antiochus Soter carried it on his victorious war banners. In India it is the emblem of Siva and Brahma; and the length of extreme silence in the Pythagorean mysteries was 5 years.

The Occult Symbols of the number 5 are—

The Magician; the Hierophant; Zeus; Nemesis.

The Hierophant is pictured seated on a throne from which show two columns each with 5 points of flame. He is bearded and crowned. In his left hand he has a triple staff, whilst the fingers of his

right hand are held with the first two bent, the
next two straight; the thumb is not seen.   At his
feet with their hands in attitude of supplication are
two men crowned: one wears a black mantle, the
other a red.   The Rosicrucian Kenneth Mackenzie
(Kenneth II.) writes concerning this number:
"This clan are associated with it, and their principal
crest is the mountain in flames."

Five as an emblem of Fire was also employed in
the Zoroastrian rites.   It is a number of fire and
struggle, competition and strife, hastiness and
anger, and of light, understanding, justice, faith,
authority, power, and will.

Therefore has it been regarded by Reincarna-
tionists as the number of re-birth, and is referred
to the 5th mansion of the heavenly map of astrology—the mansion of children, speculation, venture,
pleasure, etc.   The evils, then, are but the necessary
elements of filtration through which man is being
passed to fit him for angelhood.   In the curious
"Vision of Piers, the Plowman," the following five
sons of Conscience are given :—

See-well, Say-well, Hear-well, Work-well, and
Good-faith Go-well.

The Hebrew equivalent of the number 5 is He.

The Vibrations are Mercurial.   It is regarded as
an evil number ; Heydon classes it as indifferent.

THE NUMBER SIX

The 6th verse in the first chapter of Genesis tells
of the separation of the waters.   And man was set
on the earth by God on the 6th day to perform His
Will.   Six is regarded as the perfection of numbers

by the Quaballists and Pythagoreans, and Nico-
machus calls it Venus, to which goddess it was
sacred, and thus it is regarded as an ideal love
number. Some old writers assert that the manna
which fell in the desert for 6 days was marked with
the letter Vau, the Hebrew equivalent of the
number. In the *Sepher Yetzirah* the 6th Path
is the Mediating Influence through which infuse
the increasing emanations.

In the Quaballistic *Book of Concealed Mystery*,
the first verse of the book of Genesis is inter-
preted as " In the Beginning the substance of the
Heavens and the substance of the earth were
produced by the Elohim." Six were the created
members which are in accord with the 6 number-
ings of the Microprosopus in this wise—

(1) Benignity as his right arm.
(2) Severity as his left arm.
(3) Beauty as his body.
(4) Victory as his right leg.
(5) Glory as his left leg.
(6) Foundation as the organs of reproduction.

In the Highest Sphere 6 is indicative of the 6 letters
in the name of God.

In the Sphere of Intellect 6 indicates the 6 orders of
Angels (Seraphim, Cherubim, Thrones, Dominations, Powers, Virtues).

In the Heavenly Sphere 6 indicates the Moon and
5 planets.

In the Elemental Sphere 6 indicates the 6 elemental
qualities.

In the Lower Sphere 6 indicates the 6 degrees of
the mind.

In the Infernal Sphere 6 indicates the 6 Devils of
disaster. These are: Acteus, Megalesius, Or-
menus, Lycus, Nicon, Mimon.

The 6-pointed star (the Hexalpha) or interlaced
triangles, one pointing upwards as the triangle of
fire, the other pointing downwards as the triangle
of water, is the true seal of David and Solomon—
the " Mogan Dovid " or Shield of David. The
symbol is also emblematical of Sherkun or union
of the gods in India.

Six is a number of entanglement and binding,
of union and seduction, of vice and virtue, and
uncertainties in marriage, of love of attraction
of the sexes and of beauty. It signifies all kinds
of trouble and strife, but is capable of purification
by knowledge and a good life. Mr William Jones
relates that the Prince of Orange, who died in Paris
in 1879, and was a sporting man, always withdrew
his horses from a race in which they were classed
under number 6 or number 11. Since this state-
ment was first included in my early editions I have
been sent many theories by racing men, some of
which, though crudely expressed, contain many
occult truths. So far as I can make out, 6 is considered unlucky by some sporting men. Some
examples happen to fall on horses that have been
interfered with by the men riding them or others.
Then the idea of the 6th house in astrology—
servants, etc.—would be well carried out in the
number ; but a great mass of good evidence is
necessary before any decided opinion can be given
in a matter of this kind.

The Occult Symbols of the number 6 are—

The Lovers; the Two Paths; a Man between Virtue and Vice; Cupid with bow and arrow; the Goddess Venus.

The Man between Virtue and Vice is shown as a handsome long-haired youth, with his arms crossed on his breast and a look of indecision on his face. On his left hand is Vice in light attire urging him to travel her way; on his right hand is the angel Virtue crowned and beautiful, with hair flowing gracefully over her shoulders. She is touching the youth on the shoulder and urging him to the paths of true beauty, true love, and true majesty, for the way of right is rocky and uninviting at the entrance, but it is sublimely beautiful as the road is followed: therefore had Christian Rosy Cross to pass the allurements of the unworthy passions before illumination. Vice is delusive. She maddens her followers with a blaze of apparent beauty, which is ever in corruption and decay. Above the youth is the Spirit of Justice with shaft in bow, naked, winged, and blindfolded, issuing from the Sun. In this symbol lies the true understanding of the number 6.

The Vibrations are Venusian.

The Number Seven

On the 7th day God ended the work of Creation, and " He blessed it and sanctified it." The Bible is full of allusions to this sacred number, and students will find much in it of interest which could not be dealt with to advantage in a work of this kind, but may be later in another book.

Seven is classed as prosperous by Heydon, and it is generally so regarded. It is an entirely religious number, and as such has been esteemed by the ancients; it represents the triumph of Spirit over Matter.

When the Moon is afflicted the number is not considered fortunate, but it is considered extremely so when the Moon is in good aspect with the planets.

The 7th Path in the *Sepher Yetzirah* is that of Occult Intelligence, and represents the combination of Faith and Intellect.

In the Highest Sphere 7 is the 7-lettered name of God.

In the Sphere of Intellect 7 are the Angels before the Throne of God (Gabriel, Michael, Haniel, Raphael, Camael, Zadkiel, Zaphiel).

In the Heavenly Sphere 7 includes the 5 planets, the Sun and the Moon.

In the Elemental Sphere 7 are the planetary metals, the planetary stones, the planetary animals, the planetary birds, and the planetary fish—

The birds are the Lapwing, the Eagle, the Vulture, the Swan, the Dove, the Stork, the Owl.

The fish are the Cuttle-fish, the Dolphin, the Pike, the Whale, the Thimallus, the Mullet, the Sea-cat.

The animals are the Mole, the Hart, the Wolf, the Lion, the Goat, the Ape, the Cat.

The metals are Lead, Tin, Iron, Gold, Copper, Quicksilver, Silver.

The stones are Onyx, Sapphire, Diamond, Carbuncle, Emerald, Agate, Crystal.

In the Lower Sphere 7 are the integral members and the 7 holes of the head.

In the Infernal Sphere 7 are the infernal homes (Hell, Gates of Death, Shadow of Death, Pit of Destruction, Clay of Death, Perdition, Depth of Earth).

Francis Barrett writes as follows :—

" The Moon is the 7th of the Planets and next to us, observing this number more than the rest, this number dispensing the motion and light thereof : for in 28 days it runs round the compass of the whole Zodiac ; which number of days (the number 7 with its 7 terms) 1 to 7 doth make and fill up as much as the several numbers by adding to the antecedents, and makes 4 times 7 days in which the Moon runs through, and about, all the longitude and latitude of the Zodiac, by measuring and measuring again : with the like 7 days it dispenses its light by changing it : for the first 7 days unto the middle as it were of the divided world, it increases ; the second 7 days it fills its whole orb with light ; the third, by decreasing, is again contracted into a divided orb ; but, after the fourth 7 days it is renewed with the last diminution of its light : and by the same 7 days it disposes the increase and decrease of the sea ; for in the first 7 of the increase of the Moon it is by little and little lessened ; in the second by degrees increased ; but the third is like the first, and the fourth does the same as the second."

The Occult Symbols of the number 7 are—

" The Victor in the Chariot " ; " The Conqueror " ; " The Chariot " ; " The Cherub's Fiery Sword."

The Victor is pictured in a chariot with two columns reaching to the Heavens. It is drawn by two Sphinxes—one black and one white. The Victor stands in the chariot between the columns. He is in full armour with ornaments, representing the Moon at its increase and its decrease, on his shoulders. He holds a sceptre in his right hand, whilst his left rests upon his hip. His hair is long and curling, falling daintily on his shoulders. On his head is a crown ornamented by three golden Pentagrams. His look is serene and triumphant.

It is a number of royalty and triumph, of fame and honour, of reputation and victory. Clemens Alexandrinus notes the Lunar changes every 7 days, and the Universe was represented as a ship with 7 captains and a lion in the middle, because it was believed that the sun rose first in the celestial Lion (Leo); and John Heydon repeats the belief that a 7th son of a 7th son, if no daughter come between, can cure the "king's evil." Dr Wynn Westcott gives the following curious information relative to this number :—
" After birth, the 7th hour decides whether the child will live ; in 7 days, the cord falls off ; in twice 7 days, the eyes follow a light ; thrice 7 days, turns the head ; 7 months, gets teeth ; twice 7 months, sits firmly ; thrice 7 months, begins to talk; four times 7 months, walks strongly."

Before Shakespeare's famous " Seven Ages," an old poem, " This World is but a Vanyte," compares man's life to the 7 hours of the Roman Catholic Church, viz. : Matins, Prime, Tierce, Sext, Nones, Vespers, and Compline ; thus—" 1. Morning : The infant is like the morning, at first born, spotless and innocent. 2. Mid-morrow : This is the period of childhood. 3. Undern (9 a.m.) : The boy is put to school. 4. Midday : He is knighted and fights battles. 5. High-noon (*i.e.* nones, or 9th hour, 3 p.m.) : He is crowned a king, and fulfils all his pleasure. 6. Midovernoon (*i.e.* the middle of the period between high-noon and evensong) : The man begins to droop, and cares little for the pleasures of youth. 7. Evensong : The man walks with a staff, and death seeks him " (published about 1430 A.D.).

The Hebrew equivalent of the number 7 is Zain.
The Vibrations are Lunar.

THE NUMBER EIGHT

The number 8 is a peculiar one, and regarded as of great power by the ancient Greeks, who held that " all things are eight." When praying for Justice from Heaven we are told that Orpheus swore by the 8 deities (Fire, Water, Earth, Heaven, Moon, Sun, Phanes, Night). Circumcision, according to Jewish law, takes place on the 8th day after birth. The number is also known as the Gate of Eternity, because it succeeds the number 7. Pythagoras and his followers called 8 the number of Justice and fullness.

In the *Sepher Yetzirah* the 8th Path is the Path of Perfection.

In the Highest Sphere 8 is the 8-lettered name of God.

In the Sphere of Intellect 8 are the rewards of the blessed (Inheritance, Purity, Power, Victory, Holy Vision, Grace, Rulership, Happiness).

In the Heavenly Sphere 8 are the visible heavens
(the Star-studded Heaven, Saturn's Heaven,
Jupiter's Heaven, the Heaven of Mars, the
Sun's Heaven, the Heaven of Venus, Mercury's
Heaven, the Heaven of the Moon).

In the Elemental Sphere 8 are the qualities (Dryness
of Earth, Coldness of Water, Moisture of Air,
Heat of Fire, Heat of Air, Moisture of Water,
Dryness of Fire, Coldness of Earth).

In the Lower Sphere 8 are the virtues which attract
blessings (Peace-makers; Seekers and followers
of Truth; those that are meek; those who
suffer for Truth's sake; those Pure in Heart;
the Merciful; those who are not arrogant;
those who are TRULY sorry for the ills which
afflict the human race).

In the Infernal Sphere 8 are the rewards of the
damned (Prison, Death, Judgment, Divine
Anger, Darkness, Indignation, Tribulation,
Anguish).

John Heydon in his *Holy Guide* also mentions
the 8 blessings of the blessed and the 8 punishments
of the damned.

The Occult Symbols of the number 8 are—

Justice with the Sword and the Balance; the
Perfect Way; the 8 Priestly Ornaments (viz.
breast-plate, coat, girdle, mitre, robe, ephod,
ephod-girdle, golden plate).

Justice is seated on a throne; a sword, point
upwards, is in her right hand, and she holds
the scales in her left. Her hair is parted in
the centre, and she wears a spiked crown on her
head.

Eight is a number of attraction and repulsion, life, terrors, and all kinds of strife, of separation, disruption, destruction, promise and menace.

The Hebrew equivalent is Cheth, and the Vibrations are Saturnine.

The Number Nine

" The weird sisters, hand in hand,
Posters of the sea and land,
Thus do go about, about ;
Thrice to thine, and thrice to mine,
And thrice again, to make up nine :
Peace ! the charm's wound up."

Macbeth, Act i., Sc. 3.

The number 9 was the crooked line of the Pythagoreans, who regarded it and the number 4 as the two numerals with which is connected all intellectual, spiritual, and material knowledge. There are 9 muses, viz. : the muse of poetry, Calliope ; the muse of history, Clio ; the muse of Tragedy, Melpomene ; the muse of Music, Euterpe ; the muse of love and inspiration, Erato ; the muse of dancing, Terpsichore ; the muse of Astronomy, Urania ; the muse of comedy, Thalia ; and the muse of Eloquence, Polyhymnia. Dr Westcott writes of the Masonic Order of the " Nine Elected Knights" using 9 roses, 9 lights, and 9 knocks ; the 9 gods of the Etruscans (Juno, Minerva, Tinia, Vulcan, Mars, Saturn, Hercules, Summanus, Vedius) ; the 9 gods of the Sabines (Hercules, Romulus, Æsculapius, Bacchus, Æneas, Vesta, Santa, Fortuna, Fides). Commenting on the false rumour of the death of Pope Pius X., Monsignor Phelan is reported to have spoken as follows to a representative of the Melbourne *Herald* :—

NINE-YEAR PERIODS

" A most remarkable thing in connection with the Pope's career is that since he was ordained the various phases of his life have been divided into 9-year periods.

" The Pope was for 9 years a curate, 9 years parish priest, 9 years bishop, 9 years archbishop, 9 years Patriarch of Venice, and on August 1 he will have completed his 9th year as Pope."

The 9- and 7-year periods are peculiar in the lives of men. " The astrologers," writes Barrett, " also take notice of the number 9 in the ages of men, no otherwise than they do of 7, which they call climacterical years, which are eminent for some remarkable change."

In the *Sepher Yetzirah* the 9th Path is the Path of Pure Intelligence.

In the Highest Sphere 9 is the 9-lettered name of God.

In the Sphere of Intellect 9 are the choirs of angels and 9 are the angels ruling the heavens. The 9 choirs of angels are : Seraphim, Cherubim, Thrones, Dominations, Powers, Virtues, Principalities, Archangels, Angels. The 9 angels ruling the heavens are : Metatron, Ophaniel, Zaphkiel, Zadkiel, Camael, Raphael, Haniel, Michael, Gabriel.

In the Heavenly Sphere 9 are the movable spheres, viz.: the primum mobile ; the Star-decked Heaven ; Saturn's Sphere ; Jupiter's Sphere ; the Sphere of Mars ; the Sun's Sphere ; the Sphere of Venus ; the Sphere of Mercury ; the Sphere of the Moon.

In the Elemental Sphere 9 are the precious stones (Sapphire, Emerald, Carbuncle, Beryl, Onyx, Chrysolite, Jasper, Topaz, Sard).

In the Lower Sphere 9 are the internal and external senses (Memory, Meditation, Imagination, Common Sense, Hearing, Smelling, Seeing, Tasting, Touching).

In the Infernal Sphere 9 are the divisions of devils (False Spirits, Lying Spirits, Spirits of Iniquity, Avenging Spirits of Wickedness, Deceivers, Spirits of the Air, Furies scattering mischief, Triers or Sifters, Tempters).

The Occult Symbols of the number 9 are—

The Hermit ; Prudence Veiled, with lamp and staff ; the Cross ; the Sacred Fire curtained ; the Sacred Fire of the Vestals.

The Hermit is pictured in gown and cowl, holding out a lantern with his right hand and a staff in his left. On the ground by the end of the staff is a small snake nearly erect, such as adorned the sacred crown of the Egyptian Pharaohs and symbolised wisdom. He has a long flowing beard and an anxious thoughtful face.

The number is regarded by Heydon as very prosperous, and is generally so accepted. As a house number it is not considered fortunate, and Mr Timms has pointed out that the notorious Fleet Prison was No. 9 Fleet Street. The number is a number of the mystery and power of silence, and is connected with the astral plane. It is a number of wisdom, virtue, experience, mystery, morality, worth, rulership, human love, obscurity, protection, and the fruits of merit.

Engraved on a sard and set in a setting of silver, the number was supposed to have the property of making men invisible.

The Hebrew equivalent of the number 9 is Teth. The Vibrations are Martial.

THE NUMBER TEN

Ten has always been esteemed as a number of the Divinity, being regarded as the Hand of God. In some antique works this Hand is shown with the first and second fingers closed, the third and fourth outstretched, with the thumb beneath.

The Hebrew equivalent of the number 10 is Jod, which, say the old Rabbis (Huna and Acha), God took from the name Sarai (in Hebrew, Shin, Resh, YOD). He divided this into two parts—the Yod which is 10 into two He's or fives—giving one half to Abraham (changing the name Alef, Beth, Resh, Mem into Alef, Beth, Resh, HE, Mem) and the other half to Sarai (changing the name Shin, Resh, Yod into Shin, Resh, HE). Rabbi Joshua ben Korcha said that the Yod of Sarai went before the Holy One, praying, " O Sovereign of the Universe, why hast Thou removed me from the name of that virtuous woman ? " " Be comforted," replied God," formerly thou wert placed at the end of a woman's name, but hereafter I will give thee a place at the beginning of a man's name " ; as is written : " And Moses called He, Vau, Shin, Oyn (Joshua), the son of Nun, YOD He Shin Vau Oyn." (This I give as an example of the Quaballistical speculations of the old masters. It contains in a semi-mystical way some deep inner meanings.

These masters studied the Bible not only verse by verse, but letter by letter. Thus they succeeded in obtaining some of the secrets and much of the hidden philosophy of that Book, which is superficially criticised by some and lightly regarded by others. The true student will know that in the possession of a Bible he is rich in the possession of pearls of the greatest price. He will not seek to criticise its pages, but from them he will seek wisdom, wherein true power lies.)

The 10th Path of the *Sepher Yetzirah* is the Path of Resplendent Intelligence and the Light which, too intense for the material eye of man, is around the Throne of God.

In the Highest Sphere 10 is the 10-lettered name of God.

In the Sphere of Intellect 10 are the orders of the blessed (Blessed Souls being the extra addition) ; 10 are the angels of the Heavens (Soul of the Messiah being the extra addition).

In the Heavenly Sphere 10 are the spheres of the world (the Sphere of the Elements being the extra addition).

In the Elemental Sphere 10 are the holy animals (Dove, Lizard, Dragon, Eagle, Horse, Lion, Man, Fox, Bull, Lamb).

In the Lower Sphere 10 are the parts of man (Spirit, Brain, Spleen, Liver, Gall, Heart, Kidneys, Lungs, Genitals, Matrix).

In the Infernal Sphere 10 are the orders of the damned (Souls of the wicked ruling is the addition to 9 orders of devils).

Barrett mentions the 10 curtains of the temple,

10 strings of the psaltery, 10 musical instruments with which the psalms were sung (viz. Neza for odes; Nablum, organs; Mizmor for the psalms; Sir for the canticles; Tehila for orations; Beracha for benedictions; Halel for praises; Hodaia for thanks; Asre for happiness; Hallelujah for meditations and the praise of God alone). There are 3 decans or divisions of 10 degrees in each sign of the Zodiac, in which special planets have power according to the science of astrology. Aristotle writes that "some philosophers hold that Ideas and Numbers are of the same nature amounting to 10 in all."

The Occult Symbols of the number 10 are—

The Wheel of Fortune; Sphinx with a sword in its claws; the Hand (for the Hand of God or Yod, which is used in Jewish temples to point to the words in the reading of the law); a Circle; a Fountain; a Virgin.

The Wheel of Fortune is affixed to a staff, at the base of which are twined two serpents—a double boat on the waves carries the whole. The good genius Anubis ascends to the right of the wheel, whilst the evil genius Typhon descends to the left. At the top of the wheel is the winged Sphinx with sword in its claws.

The number is the number of Karma in the philosophy of India. It is a number of virility and manly honour, of faith and self-confidence, of rise and fall, of prophecy and futurity, of magical power, of fortune, of will, of force of necessity, of manifestation and power. The numeral 1 expresses the Universe visible, and the cypher at its side, the infinite vast which, in our finite bodies, we cannot even conceive. Dr S. L. MacGregor Mathers (Comte de Glenstrae), says "that the Hebrew Quaballists referred the highest and most abstract ideas of number" to the 10 "Emanations of Deity, for in them they recognised the key to all things." These were known as the 10 Paths of Splendour, and are The Crown, Wisdom, Understanding, Mercy, Strength and Severity, Beauty, Victory, Glory and Splendour, Foundation, Kingdom. To go into the mysteries of the Emanations would involve more technicality and detail than the limits of this book will permit.

The Vibrations of the number 10 are Solar.

The Number Eleven

The number 11 has its equivalent in the Hebrew letter Caph. Heydon classes it as prosperous, but it has not always been found so. Barrett classes it as the "number of sins and the penitent," and Westcott says that it is "a number with an evil reputation among all peoples," and just as there are 10 Paths of Splendour, so there are 11 Paths of Darkness. It was known amongst the old Jews as the number of Adam's first wife, the female devil Lilith.

In the *Sepher Yetzirah* the 11th Path is that of Glittering Intelligence, for it is held that the Path is endowed with special grandeur so that he who travels to the end of it with *true understanding* may be permitted to look upon the Face of God and live.

The Occult Symbols of the number 11 are—

A Hand Clenched ; Force (pictured by a maiden closing the jaws of a Lion) ; A Lion muzzled.

The young girl is clothed in graceful flowing robes, her long hair falls over her shoulders, and a mystic crown is on her head. She has the calm look of true understanding, and thus is able without pain or fear to close the jaws of a raging lion which crouches by her side.

Hence, 11 is a number of violence, power, bravery, energy, success in fearless ventures, liberty, the knowledge of how to " rule the stars." One cannot understand God's laws unless he studies them. Certain ills following certain set causes befall us, but if the Word of God be understood, man would know how to act when faithful action is needed. This is the secret contained in the number 11. At number 2 (1 + 1) man enters through the sacred portals ; at number 11 he begins to feel the glow of liberty.

The Vibrations of the number 11 are Lunar.

THE NUMBER TWELVE

The number 12 has its equivalent in the Hebrew letter Lamed. Heydon classes it as indifferent. It is generally regarded as a number of material suffering, although esteemed perfect and holy by the ancients, who named it " grace and perfection."

In the *Sepher Yetzirah* the 12th Path is the Path of Prophetic Vision.

The Occult Symbols of the number 12 are—

The Hanged Man ; Judas ; Prometheus Bound ; The Burnt-Offering ; The Victim.

The Hanged Man is pictured as a young man with arms bound hanging to a beam by a rope attached to his right foot. His left leg is bent to cross his right in the form of a cross. The Empress with the Orb of the World (number 3) begins to show how man may commence his lesson and so gain the Orb of the World. Sacrifice or number 12 is the first essential. Twelve is a number of trouble, experience, danger, of changes, and sadness, of knowledge, of charity, of wisdom and spiritualisation.

In Greek myth, it is related that Prometheus stole the sacred fire and was nailed to a rock in the Caucasus mountain by Hephæstus for this act, Zeus sending every day a large eagle to eat his liver, which grew again as quickly as it was consumed. The highest knowledge can only be acquired by suffering in this world of matter, and this is the meaning of the old legend which is related to the number 12. There are 12 months of the year, 12 signs of the Zodiac, 12 orders of the holy spirits, 12 angels of the heavenly divisions, 12 degrees of the damned, 12 tribes of Israel, 12 stones in the breastplate of the High Priest, 12 lions that held the brazen sea of Solomon, 12 years in which the planet Jupiter runs his course, and 12 Apostles.

The Vibrations of the number 12 are Jupiterian.

THE NUMBER THIRTEEN

The number 13 has its equivalent in the Hebrew letter Mem, and is regarded by Heydon as prosperous. It is a number of change, is not always unfortunate, as is generally supposed, although all change denotes effort, exertion, and consequent labour.

In the *Sepher Yetzirah* the 13th Path is the

Path of Unity. It is the understanding of the Truth of all Spiritual knowledge. Thus it was that the old Quaballistic masters said that " he who understands the number 13 hath the keys and power and dominion."

The Occult Symbol of the number 13 is—

A Skeleton with scythe (Death) reaping down men.

The skeleton has a scythe in his bony hands and is reaping in a field. Hands and feet are springing up amongst the leaves ; a crowned head of a man has fallen at the point of the scythe, whilst at the back of it is a female head with flowing hair parted in the centre. This is a symbol of conception and realisation. Therefore the number is a number of death, transmutation, deception, and destruction, hope, faith, and rebirth. In love affairs, it is not evil ; in marriage it is a number of harmony and happiness. It is usually supposed that it is unlucky for 13 people to sit down at a table to dine, because " 13 sat down at the Last Supper," but it seems, from Fosbroke (*Encyclopædia of Antiquities*), that the old Romans considered it an evil omen for 13 to be in a room together.

In Scandinavian mythology it is told that when the 12 great gods were seated at supper, LOKI, the god of mischief entered, quarrelled with the god of peace, BALDUR, and shot him with an arrow cut from a piece of mistletoe. The ancient Hindoos considered that it was evil for 13 to be at the same table. This superstition seems to be very universal, and is of very ancient origin. In connection with it the following story is extracted from the *Globe* (Sydney, N.S.W.) :—

WHAT HAPPENED AT AN ARTIST'S DINNER

The following anecdote is related in the biography of Sir John Millais, the famous artist. He gave a dinner in honour of Matthew Arnold in August 1885, and one of the guests called attention to the fact that there were 13 at the table, and expressed some fear. Matthew Arnold laughed at such silly superstition, and said :

" The idea is that whoever leaves the table first will die within a year ; with the permission of the ladies, we will cheat the fates for once. I and these fine, strong lads " (indicating Edgar Dawson and E— S—) " will rise together, and I think our united constitutions will be able to withstand the assault of the Reaper."

Six months later Matthew Arnold, in the prime of life, died suddenly of heart failure. A few days later E— S— was found dead in bed, a revolver by his side. Edgar Dawson, the third of the trio, sailed from Australia on February 18, 1886, and was drowned.

The same journal also states that Professor Davis, of the Indiana University, U.S.A., delivered an address to a number of school teachers recently. Thirteen is the age, he told his audience, at which 55 per cent. of the boys begin to learn evil, the age at which vices are acquired, the age from which the ruin of men dates. He based his assertion upon a critical examination of 2000 men, asking them when they first contracted such petty vices as smoking cigarettes. And of these 2000, 85 per cent. answered with the fateful word :

" Thirteen ! "

Now listen to statistics, compiled by the actuaries
of the great insurance companies of the world.   All
insurance, it should be remembered, is based upon
probabilities ;   there are tables which show how
many years a man of any given age may expect to
live ;   or, of a given number of average men, in-
discriminately gathered, how many of them have
a reasonable probability of living for a year.   These
tables are the result of averaging hundreds of thou-
sands of lives, and are mathematically accurate.
They prove this :

That of any 13 persons assembled accidentally,
or without any selection, one should be dead within
the year.   In other words, taking the population
of the world as a basis for calculation, one in every
13 persons dies each year.   The death-rate varies,
of course, according to age, climate, and sanitary
conditions.

The number was accounted sacred by the
Mexicans, the Yucatans, and many ancient people.
It is distinctly a number of regeneration, and is as
the winter which follows the autumn and precedes
the spring.   At number 4 (1 + 3) arises the Emperor
completely armed to gain his empire, which he will
do through number 13, the number of regeneration,
transformation, and spiritualisation.   Amidst the
pain of matter he who knows 13 will rise as a Victor.

The Vibrations are Solar.

THE NUMBER FOURTEEN

The number 14 has its equivalent in the Hebrew
letter Nun.   It is classed as prosperous by Heydon,
but is not generally considered so.   It is a number

of everlasting movement and combination, of
sexuality, revolution, motion, energy, indecision, temperance, trial and dangers from the
natural forces.

It is also a number of ignorance and forgetfulness,
and as such is the true number of Incarnation, the
soul descending into matter ignorant of its past
experience in the flesh. The ancient Greeks held
that the soul about to be reborn into matter drank
of the waters of Lethe, the waters of forgetfulness,
before leaving the " shades " for another pilgrimage
on earth. At number 5 (1 + 4) begins the mystery
of the Hierophant with the triple staff (Spirit, Soul,
Matter). At number 14 the struggle into matter
has commenced; the soul enters the world clothed
in its earthly dress. Here begins the work of the
magician.

In the *Sepher Yetzirah* the 14th Path is the
Path of Sanctity and Preparation.

The Occult Symbols of the number 14 are—

Temperance; The Two Ewers; The Mutilated
Osiris.

Egyptian mythology tells that after Set had
slain Osiris he cut the body into 14 parts.

Temperance is pictured as a beautiful winged
girl with a star on her forehead. She pours liquid
from an ewer of gold into an ewer of silver without
the loss of a drop.

The Vibrations are Mercurial.

The Number Fifteen

The number 15 has its equivalent in the Hebrew
letter Samek. It is classed by Heydon as in-

different, and is generally regarded as evil. It is, however, a number of occult significance, of magic and mystery, and the understanding of it leads to great spiritual heights.

In the *Sepher Yetzirah* the 15th Path is the Path of Darkness.

The Occult Symbols of the number 15 are—

"THE DEVIL"

Eliphas Levi also includes " The Goat of Mendes " and " The Baphomet of the Templars."

The Devil is standing on a cube, to which are chained two smaller devils—(one male, another female). In his right hand he holds the candle of Black Magic, in his left a ring. He has the Wings of Evil, is horned and long-eared. His face is like a goat, and he has goats' legs and hoofs.

The number 15 was, in the Middle Ages, associated with the weird and unholy Witches' Sabbath, and does not represent the highest side of magic. It is a number of eloquence, fatality, marriage, troubles, and voluptuousness.

It represents the temptation of man, and is compared to the Dweller on the Threshold (Nahash) introduced into Lord Lytton's Rosicrucian romance *Zanoni*. At number 6 (1 + 5) arises the man between Virtue and Vice. At number 15 Vice opens before him in hideous reality. If his soul be weak, he will be engulfed.

The Vibrations are Venusian.

THE NUMBER SIXTEEN

The number 16 has its equivalent in the Hebrew letter Ayin. It is classed by Heydon as very

good, but its influence is generally found to be
bad.

In the *Sepher Yetzirah* the 16th Path is the
Path of Glory and Victory for the Righteous.

The Occult Symbols of the number 16 are—
"THE LIGHTNING-STRUCK TOWER,"
"The Shattered Citadel," and "The Tower of
Babel Blasted."

A shaft of Lightning has shattered a strong tower
from which are falling two men, one of whom has
a crown on his head.

At number 7 (1 + 6) arises the Victor, who at
number 16 is threatened with fatality and has to
pass his first great trial.

Sixteen is a number of weakness and subversion,
accidents and catastrophes, defeat and danger.

Its Vibrations are Lunar.

THE NUMBER SEVENTEEN

The number 17 has its equivalent in the Hebrew
letter Pé. It is classed by Heydon as very good,
and so it has always been found to be. It is a very
spiritual number, and is symbolised as
"THE STAR,"
"The Burning Star," "The Star of the Magi."

Eliphas Levi uses the following beautiful symbol :
"A naked woman, representing Truth, Nature,
and Wisdom unveiled, inclines two urns towards
the earth, and pours out fire and water upon it ;
above her head glitters the Septenary, circling
round an 8-pointed star, that of Venus ; symbol
of peace and love."

In the *Sepher Yetzirah* the 17th Path is the Path

of the Realisation and Reward of the Righteous,
for here is their Faith rewarded with the mantle
of the Holy Spirit.

This number is one of immortality, moral influence of the idea or forms, flow of thought,
uncertainty, intuition, expression, clairvoyance,
beauty, and hope.

In ancient Egypt 17 was considered unholy,
because it was on the 17th day of the moon that
Osiris was slain.

At number 8 (1 + 7) arises the perfect path of
Justice which at number 17 reaches the guiding
star of the Magi.

The Vibrations are Saturnine.

THE NUMBER EIGHTEEN

The number 18 has its equivalent in the Hebrew
letter Tzaddi.   Heydon classes it as indifferent, but
it is always bad.   The Occult Symbols are—
"THE MOON,"
The Twilight, The Falling Dew, The Blood-stained
Path.

From a rayed moon, a rain of blood is dropping
on to a field between two towers.   A wolf and a
dog are catching some drops of blood in their
opened mouths ; from below is a crab hastening
to join them.   This is symbolic of the world of
materialism striving to destroy the soul.

In the *Sepher Yetzirah* the 18th Path is the Path
of the Senses.

Eighteen is a number of the elements, reflected
light, treachery, and deception, troubles in love,
error, bad judgment, and evil associations.

At number 9 (1 + 8) the Hermit sets out with his lantern to find the path of holiness; at number 18 he enters the twilight; the way is blood-stained, and treachery and deception surround him.

The Vibrations are Martial.

The Number Nineteen

The number 19 has its equivalent in the Hebrew letter Qoph. Heydon classes it as very good, and it is generally so regarded. It is symbolised as
" The Sun,"
" The Prince of Heaven," " An Angel Unwinding Destinies," " A Naked Child on a Snow-white Horse, holding a Scarlet Standard."

The Sun throws his rays mingled with drops of liquid gold on two little naked children—a girl and a boy. Behind is a stone wall. This is emblematic of the arising of the man who has pierced the material world, and begins to understand his link with God and the worlds, Divine and Material.

In the *Sepher Yetzirah* the 19th Path is the Path of Spiritual Activity.

Nineteen is a number of happiness, vanity, good fortune in marriage, success, esteem, and honour.

At number 1 the beautiful magician sets forth with a smile of hope to accomplish his mission; at number 10 he grasps fortune's wheel; he prophesies, and enters the paths of wisdom; at number 19 (1 + 9 = 10 ; 1 + 0 = 1) he enters the spiritual paths and unites himself with God.

The Vibrations are Solar.

THE NUMBER TWENTY

The number 20 has its equivalent in the Hebrew letter Resh. It is classed by Heydon as very good. It is a peculiar number, and its exact potency is a matter of doubt. It is symbolised as
"THE LAST JUDGMENT,"
" The Angel," and " The Awakening of the Dead."

The Angel is winged and surrounded by rays ; a halo is round her head ; on her forehead is a star. She sounds the judgment-trumpet, to which is attached a flag bearing a cross. From a tomb in the earth arise a man, a woman, and a child, their hands clasped together in attitude of prayer. Hence is the awakening.

Twenty is a number of life and impulse, of obstacles, fatalities, hindrances, decisions, and exaltation.

In the *Sepher Yetzirah* the 20th Path is the Path of Primordial Wisdom and its diffusion.

At number 2 man enters the sacred portals ; at number 11 he begins to feel the glow of liberty ; at number 20 $(2 + 0 = 2)$ he ascends to the knowledge of spiritual freedom, and the shades of materialism fall from his eyes.

The Vibrations are Lunar.

THE NUMBER TWENTY-ONE

The number 21 has its equivalent in the Hebrew letter Shin. It is classed by Heydon as indifferent. It is certainly peculiar, being the number of absolute Truth, and the smallest particle of truth is never gained without a very big sacrifice. To gaze upon this holy light, true men have dared torture, contumely, and hate, and though this has forced them from the earth, the circumstances of their deaths have caused a little brighter ray of precious truth to flicker on the world. Twenty-one is symbolised as

"THE UNIVERSE,"
" Truth in the Middle of a Crown, holding a Magic Wand in Her Hands," and "The Crown of the Magi."

A graceful woman, nude save for a flowing scarf, stands in the centre of a cone of leaves, her left leg across her right in the form of a cross. In her left hand she holds a magic wand, in her right the end of the scarf. At the bottom of the cone are a bull and a lion, at the top an eagle and a winged man (the 4 Apocalyptic animals). To gain the world 21 $(2 + 1 = 3)$, the Empress (3) has passed the gate of sacrifice (12).

In the *Sepher Yetzirah* the 21st Path is the Path of Conciliation, whence reflect the Blessings of God upon the world.

Twenty-one is a number of truth, honour, hope, advancement, elevation, and success. But it must not be forgotten that to gain the excellent promises of this number unyielding energy is an absolute essential.

The Vibrations are Jupiterian.

THE NUMBER TWENTY-TWO

The number 22 has its equivalent in the Hebrew letter Tau. Heydon classes it as very good ; why, I do not know, because its action has been found always to be evil, so far as earth matters are concerned. It is symbolised as

"THE FOOL,"

and "A Blind Man in Fool's Dress, with a Knapsack full of Errors. He offers no defence against a ferocious tiger who is biting him."

In the *Sepher Yetzirah* the 22nd Path is the Path whence the holy spiritual lights stream forth over the denizens of the earth. The Emperor (number 4) travels through the paths of transformation (number 13) and enters the illusion of matter.

Twenty-two is a number of error and folly, false judgment and the consequence, imprisonment or restraint, accidents, arrogance, and catastrophe.

The Vibrations are Solar.

THE NUMBER TWENTY-THREE

This number is classed as very good by Heydon, and so it is generally found to be. In Quaballistic astrology it is symbolised as the

"ROYAL STAR OF THE LION."

It is a number of success, help from superiors, protection from people of position, fame.

In the *Sepher Yetzirah* the 23rd path is the Path of Stability. At number 14 the Hierophant (5) has fully commenced his struggle with matter; at number 23 he reaches the Royal Star of Leo and rises above mere sensation.

The Vibrations are Mercurial.

THE NUMBER TWENTY-FOUR

This number is classed by Heydon as very bad, but it is usually found to be fairly good. No symbol can be found to relate to it, but it gives the aid and association of people of quality, and gain through influential women.

Dr Westcott points out that it is the number of Cain, although it is "not of his numeration." It is possibly for this reason that Heydon accounts 24 evil.

In the *Sepher Yetzirah* the 24th Path is the Path of Imaginative Intelligence.

The Vibrations are Venusian.

The Number Twenty-Five

This number is classed by Heydon as "very bad." The reason is not clear. It is generally found to be fairly good, although somewhat of a struggling indication. No symbol is given.

It is a number of strength gained by experience, gain through strife, benefits from observation, elevation and support, effect and cause.

In the *Sepher Yetzirah* the 25th Path is the Path of Trial, for from this path God tries man even as He tried Abraham.

The Vibrations are Lunar.

The Number Twenty-Six

Heydon classes this number as "very good," possibly because it "is the number of Jehovah." It is almost always found to be evil, and is a number of disaster, ruin by injudicious speculations, bad partnerships, greed, and struggle. No symbol is given.

In the *Sepher Yetzirah* the 26th Path is the Path of Renewing Intelligence.

The Vibrations are Saturnine.

THE NUMBER TWENTY-SEVEN

Heydon is right in regarding this number as " very good." It is symbolised in Quaballistic astrology as " The Sceptre," and is, as the symbol shows, a number of authority and power. It indicates the fruits of a productive intellect, fortunate undertakings, much success, and beneficial works.

In the *Sepher Yetzirah* the 27th Path is the Path wherein is created the mighty Intellect of all created things.

Its Vibrations are Martial.

THE NUMBER TWENTY-EIGHT

This number is classed by Heydon as " very bad," and it is generally so regarded. No symbol is given.

It is a number of disaster, evil connections, unwariness, oppositions, injuries in trade and contention, loss of the results of work, and various annoyances.

In the *Sepher Yetzirah* the 28th Path is the Path wherein the natures of all created beings are perfected.

The Vibrations are Solar.

THE NUMBER TWENTY-NINE

This number is not what is known as a distinct potency. It is classed by Heydon as " very bad." It must be reduced to a potency when dealing with it practically. To find this, we must add the two numbers together; thus 29 equals 2 plus 9 equals 11; therefore, the number is transformed into 11, and as 11 it must be regarded.

In the *Sepher Yetzirah* the 29th Path is the Path whence all bodies are formed.

The Vibrations are Lunar.

The Number Thirty

This number Heydon classes as very bad; but as it is not a distinct potency it must be reduced to find its meaning—as before, 30 equals 3 plus 0 equals 3; therefore the number must be regarded as 3, not 30.

In the *Sepher Yetzirah* the 30th Path is the Path whence astrologers deduce their judgments.

The Vibrations are Jupiterian.

The Number Thirty-One

This number is powerful, and the number of the Lord, but not being a distinct potency it must be reduced to its potency; thus 3 plus 1 equals 4, to which the student must refer.

In the *Sepher Yetzirah* the 31st Path regulates the Solar and Lunar movements.

The Vibrations are Solar.

The Number Thirty-Two

This number is magical, but not being a distinct potency we must reduce it; thus 3 plus 2 equals 5, to which number the student is referred.

In the *Sepher Yetzirah* the last and 32nd Path regulates the movements of the Planets.

The Vibrations are Mercurial.

In the same manner and for the same reason—

THIRTY-THREE equals 33 equals 3 plus 3 equals 6—Vibrations Venusian
THIRTY-FOUR   „   34   „   3 „   4   „   7   „   Lunar
THIRTY-FIVE   „   35   „   3 „   5   „   8   „   Saturnine
THIRTY-SIX   „   36   „   3 „   6   „   9   „   Martial

THE NUMBER THIRTY-SEVEN

This is a distinct potency, and is symbolised as
" THE ROYAL STAR OF THE BULL."

It is a number of goodwill, success, and pleasant achievements, and is fortunate in friendship, in love and marriage, in partnerships and combinations, and in matters connected with the fair sex.

It is the most fortunate of the 10 potencies, 3 plus 7 equals 10 ; but is distinct in itself.

The Vibrations are Solar.

THIRTY-EIGHT equals 38 equals 3 plus 8 equals 11—Vibrations Lunar
THIRTY-NINE   „   39   „   3 „   9   „   12   „   Jupiterian
FORTY   „   40   „   4 „   0   „   4   „   Solar
FORTY-ONE   „   41   „   4 „   1   „   5   „   Mercurial
FORTY-TWO   „   42   „   4 „   2   „   6   „   Venusian

THE NUMBER FORTY-THREE

This is a very bad number.   It is symbolised as
" THE DEATH POINT."

It is a number of upheaval and strife, destruction and failure, frustration.

The Vibrations are Lunar.

FORTY-FOUR equals 44 equals 4 plus 4 equals 8—Vibrations Saturnine
FORTY-FIVE   „   45   „   4 „   5   ,   9   „   Martial
FORTY-SIX   „   46   „   4 „   6   „ 10   „   Solar
FORTY-SEVEN   „   47   „   4 „   7   „ 11   „   Lunar
FORTY-EIGHT   „   48   „   4 „   8   „ 12   „   Jupiterian
FORTY-NINE   „   49   „   4 „   9   „ 13   „   Solar
FIFTY   „   50   „   5 „   0   „   5   „   Mercurial

The Number Fifty-One

A peculiar number, symbolised as
"The Royal Star of the Waterman,"
indicating a warlike nature, enemies and danger,
but sudden advancement. A military number.

The Vibrations are Venusian.

Fifty-two	equals	52	equals	5	plus	2	equals	7—Vibrations	Lunar
Fifty-three	,,	53	,,	5	,,	3	,,	8	,,	Saturnine
Fifty-four	,,	54	,,	5	,,	4	,,	9	,,	Martial

The Number Fifty-Five

This number is symbolised as
"The Sword."

This is a victorious symbol signifying energy and
triumph. But the sword is aggressive as well as
protective, and he who takes it up may perish by it.
The number is, however, an important and magical
number. It denotes mental penetration which
pierces the darkness of ignorance as a sharp sword
pierces a dense body.

The Vibrations are Solar.

Fifty-six	equals	56	equals	5	plus	6	equals	11—Vibrations	Lunar
Fifty-seven	,,	57	,,	5	,,	7	,,	12	,,	Jupiterian
Fifty-eight	,,	58	,,	5	,,	8	,,	13	,,	Solar
Fifty-nine	,,	59	,,	5	,,	9	,,	14	,,	Mercurial
Sixty	,,	60	,,	6	,,	0	,,	6	,,	Venusian
Sixty-one	,,	61	,,	6	,,	1	,,	7	,,	Lunar
Sixty-two	,,	62	,,	6	,,	2	,,	8	,,	Saturnine
Sixty-three	,,	63	,,	6	,,	3	,,	9	,,	Martial
Sixty-four	,,	64	,,	6	,,	4	,,	10	,,	Solar

The Number Sixty-Five

This is the "number of Adonai," and a holy
number therefore. Its symbol is
"The Royal Star of the Scorpion,"
and it gives powerful patrons and a happy marriage.

It is, however, a number of hurts and dangers.
The Vibrations are Lunar.

SIXTY-SIX	equals 12—Vibrations	Jupiterian
SIXTY-SEVEN	„ 13	„	Solar
SIXTY-EIGHT	„ 14	„	Mercurial

THE NUMBER SIXTY-NINE

Is a number of fortune, honour, and fame.   It is
symbolised as
"THE CROWN OF MARS."
The Vibrations are Venusian.

THE NUMBER SEVENTY

Is a fortunate number, but not a distinct potency;
therefore its power must be found in the same way
as the others;   70 equals 7 plus 0 equals 7.
The Vibrations are Lunar.

THE NUMBER SEVENTY-ONE

This is a powerful number, but not altogether
fortunate, as it threatens the body and the worldly
concerns.   It is symbolised as
"THE REAPER."
The Vibrations are Saturnine.

THE NUMBER SEVENTY-TWO

Is a number of the Angels and of Mercy.   Still,
as it is not a distinct potency, its power is in the
number 9.
The Vibrations are Martial.

THE NUMBER SEVENTY-THREE

Is a number of Wisdom, having its power in the number 10.

The Vibrations are Solar.

The planetary numbers of the Divine Names are given by Francis Barrett as follows :—

Saturn, 3, 9, 15, 45.   Venus, 7, 49, 175, 1225.

Jupiter, 4, 16, 34, 136.   Mercury, 8, 64, 260, 2080.

Mars, 5, 25, 65, 325.   Moon, 9, 81, 369, 3321.

Sun, 6, 36, 111, 666.

Dr MacGregor Mathers (Comte de Glenstrae) gives similarly the numbers appropriate to the planets. They are given by John Heydon from ancient sources, as follows :—

Sun, 1 and 4.   Venus, 6.

Moon, 2 and 7.   Saturn, 8.

Jupiter, 3.   Mars, 9.

Mercury, 5.

The latter author numbers the Zodiacal Constellations from ancient sources as—

Aries 7, Taurus 6, Gemini 12, Cancer 5, Leo 1, Virgo 10, Libra 8, Scorpio 9, Sagittarius 4, Capricorn 3, Aquarius 2, Pisces 11.

ODD AND EVEN NUMBERS

It is said that odd numbers are fortunate, an assertion which probably arose because the odd numbers are assigned to the greater and more powerful gods, and the even numbers to the lesser ones. We will now tabulate the odd and even numbers from 1 to 73, and so see at a glance the power allotted to each.

Odd	*Even*
1. Fortunate	2. Unfortunate
3. Fortunate	4. Fortunate
5. Unfortunate	6. Unfortunate
7. Fortunate	8. Unfortunate
9. Doubtful (tendency fortunate)	10. Fortunate
11. Doubtful (tendency unfortunate)	12. Unfortunate
13. Doubtful (tendency unfortunate)	14. Unfortunate
15. Unfortunate	16. Unfortunate
17. Fortunate	18. Unfortunate
19. Fortunate	20. Doubtful (tendency fortunate)
21. Doubtful (tendency fortunate)	22. Unfortunate
23. Fortunate	24. Fortunate
25. Fortunate	26. Unfortunate
27. Fortunate	28. Unfortunate
29. Unfortunate	30. Doubtful (tendency fortunate)
31. Fortunate	32. Unfortunate
33. Unfortunate	34. Fortunate
35. Unfortunate	36. Doubtful (tendency fortunate)
37. Fortunate	38. Unfortunate
39. Unfortunate	40. Fortunate
41. Unfortunate	42. Unfortunate
43. Unfortunate	44. Unfortunate
45. Doubtful (tendency fortunate)	46. Fortunate
47. Unfortunate	48. Unfortunate

49. Unfortunate
51. Unfortunate
53. Unfortunate

55. Fortunate
57. Unfortunate
59. Unfortunate
61. Fortunate
63. Doubtful (tendency fortunate)
65. Unfortunate
67. Unfortunate
69. Unfortunate
71. Unfortunate
73. Fortunate

50. Unfortunate
52. Fortunate (Weak)
54. Doubtful (tendency fortunate)
56. Unfortunate
58. Unfortunate
60. Unfortunate
62. Unfortunate
64. Fortunate

66. Unfortunate
68. Unfortunate
70. Fortunate
72. Doubtful (tendency fortunate)

Of the Odds—

13 numbers are classed as Fortunate.

18　,,　,,　,,　,, Unfortunate.

5　,,　,,　,,　,, Doubtful, but of fortunate tentencies.

1 number is　,,　,, Doubtful, but of unfortunate tendencies.

Of the Evens—

9 numbers are classed as Fortunate.

22　,,　,,　,,　,, Unfortunate.

5　,,　,,　,,　,, Doubtful with fortunate tendencies.

The greater number of fortunate numbers are therefore amongst the odds.

The numbers 9, 12, 13, and 22 are the worst house numbers.

It must be well understood that all numbers, no matter how large, must be reduced to a potency ; for example, several people failed in business in premises bearing the number 328. 328 equals 3 plus 2 plus 8 equals 13—a doubtful point, and a bad house number. Of the three numerals composing the entire—3 is good, 2 and 8 are evil. We shall have examples more sensational than this, however, in the succeeding chapter.

CHAPTER II

NUMERICAL VALUE OF THE LETTERS

To every Hebrew letter a number was allotted, and by virtue of this transposition many wonderful things could be done by the scholars of old who made remarkable prognostications from this procedure solely. Careful study will convince the searcher of the amount of wisdom which can be obtained by the knowledge of the mystic property of numbers. It is related that that remarkable, though now much abused, man, Count Cagliostro, won huge sums at the Paris gaming tables by his skill in this branch of Quaballistic art. Three distinct times he told the Baroness de la Motte the winning numbers in the Paris lotteries, but declined to tell her a fourth time on the grounds that he had already given her enough information to make three fortunes with. It is an old custom of the Jews to change the name of a person sick unto death in the hope that by this act better conditions will be brought about for the material welfare of the sufferer, the old Rabbinical philosophy agreeing that the four things necessary to annul destiny's evil decree were prayer, charity, CHANGE OF NAME, and change of actions. Dr S.

L. MacGregor Mathers (Comte de Glenstrae) has erected the following table of Hebrew letter values, with their English equivalents :—

Aleph	equals	A	equals	1
Beth	,,	Bh. B	,,	2
Gimel	,,	Gh. G	,,	3
Daleth	,,	Dh. D	,,	4
He	,,	H.E	,,	5
Vau	,,	V.U	,,	6
Zain	,,	Z	,,	7
Cheth	,,	Ch (guttural as in the German Hoch)	,,	8
Teth	,,	T	,,	9
Yod	,,	I.Y	,,	10
Kaph	,,	Kh. K	,,	20
Lamed	,,	L	,,	30
Mem	,,	M	,,	40
Nun	,,	N	,,	50
Samekh	,,	S	,,	60
Ayin	,,	Ngh (Guttural)	,,	70
Pé	,,	Ph. P	,,	80
Tzaddi	,,	Tz	,,	90
Qoph	,,	Qh. Q	,,	100
Resh	,,	Rh. R	,,	200
Shin	,,	Sh. S	,,	300
Tau	,,	Th. T	,,	400

The finals are—Final Kaph 500, Final Mem 600, Final Nun 700, Final Pé 800, Final Tzaddi 900.

It will be found, however, more expedient to employ the following condensed table for all ordinary purposes :—

A equals 1	B equals 2	G equals 3	D equals 4
I ,, 1	C ,, 2	L ,, 3	M ,, 4
J ,, 1	K ,, 2	S ,, 3	T ,, 4
Q ,, 1	R ,, 2		
Y ,, 1			
E ,, 5	U ,, 6	O ,, 7	F ,, 8
N ,, 5	V ,, 6	Z ,, 7	H ,, 8 or 5
X ,, 5	W ,, 6		P ,, 8
H ,, 5 or 8			

In the earlier editions of this work the letter X was classed under 6. It has rather, I think, a K.S sound, and I prefer to allot to it the number 5. The letter H is grouped under 8 in the earlier editions, but I am of opinion that its value is *generally* 5, except when the sound is harsh.

It is now desirable that I should explain in what manner the above can be put to practical use, and I cannot better do so than by subjoining a number of examples in illustration. Napoleon originally spelt his name as Napoleon Buonaparte ; he changed it into Napoleon Bonaparte. We will consider these names with the aid of our Quaballistic searchlight.

Napoleon equals 41 equals 4 plus 1 equals 5
Buonaparte ,, 41 ,, 4 ,, 1 ,, 5

—

10

Number 5 as explained in the previous pages is symbolised as—

"THE MAGICIAN"

a number of fire and struggle, competition and

strife, hastiness and anger, and of light, understanding, and justice.

The combined names are contained in the number
10, symbolised as—

"THE WHEEL OF FORTUNE,"

a number of virility, of faith and self-confidence,
of rise and fall, of prophecy and futurity, of manifestation and power.

Now we are told that Napoleon struck out the
letter u from his surname, thereby making it
Bonaparte.   Let us see what effect this will
have.

Napoleon equals 41 equals 4 plus 1 equals 5
Bonaparte   „   35   „   3   „   5   „   8
                                                      —
                                                      13

We have considered the name Napoleon.   The
surname Bonaparte totals to 8.

Number 8 is symbolised as—

"JUSTICE WITH THE SWORD AND BALANCE,"

a number of attraction and repulsion, life, terror,
and all kinds of strife, of separation, disruption,
destruction, promise, and menace.

The combined names are contained in the number
13, symbolised as—

"DEATH,"

a skeleton with scythe, reaping down men;   a
number of death, deception, and destruction.

These sensational results, so in agreement with
all that is known of Napoleon, are neither obtained
by chance nor guesswork, as the following explana-
tion clearly proves :—

N equals 5		B equals 2		B equals 2	
A	,, 1	U	,, 6	O	,, 7
P	,, 8	O	,, 7	N	,, 5
O	,, 7	N	,, 5	A	,, 1
L	,, 3	A	,, 1	P	,, 8
E	,, 5	P	,, 8	A	,, 1
O	,, 7	A	,, 1	R	,, 2
N	,, 5	R	,, 2	T	,, 4
	—	T	,, 4	E	,, 5
	41	E	,, 5		—
			—		35
			41		

As neither 41 nor 35 are distinct potencies, they must be reduced to their lowest Quaballistic equivalent, as explained in Chap. I. This it will be seen I have done.

We will now take as another example the Empress Josephine :—

J equals 1		B equals 2	
O	,, 7	E	,, 5
S	,, 3	A	,, 1
E	,, 5	U	,, 6
P	,, 8	H	,, 5
H	,, 5	A	,, 1
I	,, 1	R	,, 2
N	,, 5	N	,, 5
E	,, 5	A	,, 1
	—	I	,, 1
	40	S	,, 3
			—
			32

Forty is not a distinct potency, then 4 plus 0 equals 4 equals The Emperor, The Cubic Stone, etc.

Thirty-two is not a distinct potency, then 3 plus 2 equals 5 equals The Magician, Nemesis, etc., and 4 plus 5 equals 9 equals The Hermit, The Sacred Fire Curtained, etc.

Josephine realises her hopes (Number 4) by her marriage with the Emperor; Beauharnais is the Magician who gains power and authority but is unable to hold it—hence Nemesis. The combined names equal 9—the Lamp that is Veiled; the number of experience and obscurity.

If we regard H as 8 instead of 5, then we shall have 43 for Josephine and 35 equals 3 plus 5 equals 8 for Beauharnais; then 43 plus 5 equals 48 equals 12 equals The Sacrifice. Was Josephine sacrificed? That her lamp was veiled and that she fell from elevation to obscurity is known.

Now let us take the names of a number of ships which disaster has overtaken during the last few years. I am, of course, confining my remarks generally to ships with English names, for we are dealing with an English Quaballah constructed from the original Hebrew.

The greatest shipping disaster the world has seen is, without doubt, the wreck of the TITANIC: the very horror of it all is fresh within our minds. According to a lady survivor, this great liner, one of the triumphs of the shipbuilders' art, found its grave in the icy waters, "pressed down as if by invisible hands." The name Titanic equals 18, thus :—

T equals 4
I   „   1
T   „   4
A   „   1
N   „   5
I   „   1
C   „   2
———
18

18 is an evil number. "The Twilight," "The Blood-Stained Path"—a number of the elements, deception, bad judgment, etc.

Another recent disaster was the loss of the WARATAH, which sank with all hands. This name equals W 6, A 1, R 2, A 1, T 4, A 1, H 5 equals 20, "The Last Judgment,"—a number of obstacles and fatalities.

Another was the TEXAS, equals T 4, E 5, X 5, A 1, S 3, equals 18, the same as the Titanic.

Another was the KOOMBANA, lost with all hands, equals K 2, O 7, O 7, M 4, B 2, A 1, N 5, A 1, equals 29—an evil number equals 11, A Muzzled Lion—a number of violence, etc.

Another was the OCEANA equals O 7, C 2, E 5, A 1, N 5, A 1, equals 21—a number of sacrifice.

Another was the DELHI, equals D 4, E 5, L 3, H 5, I 1, equals 18—the same as the Titanic.

The list published in the early editions may be repeated here, revised :—

U.S. Warship MAINE equals M 4, A 1, I 1, N 5, E 5, equals 16—an evil number, "The Lightning-Struck Tower," "The Shattered Citadel," etc.

H.M.S. COBRA equals C 2, O 7, B 2, R 2, A 1, equals 14—an evil number. Symbol—"The Two Ewers." The vessel broke in halves.

H.M.S. VIPER equals V 6, I 1, P 8, E 5, R 2, equals 22—an evil number. Symbol—"A Blind Man in a Fool's Dress," etc. It is a number of error, false judgment and the consequences, catastrophe.

H.M.S. CRANE equals C 2, R 2, A 1, N 5, E 5, equals 15—an evil number. Symbol—"The Devil." A number of fatality.

Steam Trawler CRANE, sunk by the Russians equals 15 also. (Note the same evil name.)

H.M.S. SERPENT equals S 3, E 5, R 2, P 8, E 5, N 5, T 4, equals 32 equals 3 plus 2 equals 5—an evil point.

H.M.S. BRAZEN equals B 2, R 2, A 1, Z 7, E 5, N 5, equals 22.

H.M.S. SULTAN equals S 3, U 6, L 3, T 4, A 1, N 5, equals 22.

H.M.S. CAPTAIN equals C 2, A 1, P 8, T 4, A 1, I 1, N 5, equals 22.

This vessel, an iron-turret ship, capsized during a squall near Finisterre, 7th September 1870, and 469 brave sailors perished.

Troopship BIRKENHEAD equals B 2, I 1, R 2, K 2, E 5, N 5, H 5, E 5, A 1, D 4, equals 32, not a direct potency, therefore 3 plus 2 equals 5—an evil number.

I mention the Birkenhead in this list because the sensation caused by her loss and the loss of the greater part of her company in 1852 has not subsided even to-day, when we remember with admiration the heroic soldiers and sailors who stood as on parade on the deck of the ill-fated ship smiling at death.

S.S. ROYAL CHARTER equals R 2, O 7, Y 1, A 1, L 3, C 2, H 5, A 1, R 2, T 4, E 5, R 2, equals 35 —a doubtful number, but not a distinct potency, equals 3 plus 5 equals 8—a number of terror and destruction.

H.M.S. WASP equals W 6, A 1, S 3, P 8, equals 18—an evil number.   Symbols—"The Moon," "The Twilight," etc.   A number of error and bad judgment.   This vessel was wrecked off Tory Island in 1884.   Cause stated : "Error in navigation."

H.M.S. WASP.—This Wasp was lost with all hands in the China Seas in 1887.

H.M.S. ROYAL GEORGE.—R 2, O 7, Y 1, A 1, L 3, G 3, E 5, O 7, R 2, G 3, E 5, equals 39 equals 3 plus 9 equals 12—an evil point.   "The Victim," etc.   The history of the loss of this vessel with Admiral Kempenfelt and 900 men, 29th August 1782, is too well known to need repetition here.

R.M.S. SIMLA equals 12—an evil number.

R.M.S. AUSTRALIA equals 22—an evil number.

R.M.S. ORIZABA equals 21—a doubtful number.

I think it scarcely necessary to continue the list any further.   The examples given will enable anyone to understand the methods applied.   The names are selected haphazard, and the results, it must be admitted, are significant enough, although it sometimes will happen that a fortunate captain will be a potent influence for the good and salvation of an unfortunate ship and *vice versa*, for many a fine vessel successful in very many voyages has met with disaster when under the charge of a new skipper. It seems significant that the three " reptile " warships, the COBRA, the VIPER, and the SERPENT, should all prove unfortunate.

CHAPTER III

THE QUABALLAH OF PYTHAGORAS

THERE are several systems of valuations set down to the mystic Pythagoras, who flourished about 580–570 B.C. He was born in the island of Samos, and was from an early age a student of the occult arts. He travelled into Egypt and was initiated into the mysteries of the priests of that famous land of the Pharaohs, an exclusive honour not usually bestowed upon a foreigner. He formed a school of mystic philosophy in the lovely Greek city of Southern Italy, Crotona, and is believed to have died at Metapontum. He held that " numbers are the principles of all things ; that the universe is a harmonious whole (Kosmos), the heavenly bodies by their motions causing sounds (music of the spheres) ; that the soul is immortal and passes successively through many bodies (metempsychosis) ; and that the highest aim and blessedness of man is likeness to the Deity." The system which I give now has a 9 potency, and presents many points of difference from the preceding ; the letters are valued as follows :—

A equals 1	K equals 10	T equals 100	
B „ 2	L „ 20	U „ 200	W equals double V
C „ 3	M „ 30	X „ 300	„ 1400
D „ 4	N „ 40	Y „ 400	
E „ 5	O „ 50	Z „ 500	
F „ 6	P „ 60	J „ 600	
G „ 7	Q „ 70	V „ 700	
H „ 8	R „ 80	Hi. „ 800	
I „ 9	S „ 90	Hv. „ 900	

The 9 potency, of which I have spoken, is clearly shown in the above table. A to I is 1 to 9, K to S is 10 to 90, T to Hv. is 100 to 900. Now, before proceeding further, let us consider the import of the numbers as usually accepted.

TABLE OF INTERPRETATION

1. Ambition, Intention, Passion.
2. Death, Destruction, Fatality.
3. Destiny, Faith, The Soul, Religion.
4. Strength, Power, Wisdom, Solidity.
5. Marriage, Pleasure, Happiness, The Stars.
6. Perfected Labour.
7. Ideal Happiness, Freedom, Rest, Way of Life.
8. Protection, Justice.
9. Anxiety, Imperfection, Grief.
10. Logic, Success, Happiness to Come.
11. Inharmony, Slight Offences, Punishment, Equivocation.
12. Good Signature (also a town or city).
13. Unrighteousness.
14. Sacrifice.
15. Goodness, Self-Culture, Piety.
16. Sensuality, Luxury, Love, Happiness.
17. Misfortune, Carelessness, Forgetfulness.

18. Wickedness, Hardness of Heart.
19. Imbecility, Folly.
20. Wisdom, Sadness, Austerity.
21. Wisdom, Mystery, Creation.
22. Divine Vengeance, Chastisement.
23. Ignorance of the Justice of God, Prejudice.
24. Travels.
25. Mind, Intelligence, The Birth of Children.
26. Good Works, The Humanitarian.
27. Bravery, Firmness.
28. Love and Love Gifts.
29. News.
30. Fame, Marriage.
31. Love of Fame, Virtue.
32. Marriage.
33. Purity and Grace.
34. Karma, Suffering, Troubles.
35. Sweetness, Health, Peace.
36. Genius, Great Understanding.
37. Faithfulness, Conjugal Felicity.
38. Malice, Greed, Imperfection.
39. Honour, Praise.
40. Holidays, Festivals, A Wedding.
41. Shame, Disgrace.
42. A Brief and Miserable Life.
43. The Temple, Religion, Worship.
44. Kingly Power, Elevation, Pomp, Ceremony.
45. Children, Issue, Population.
46. Fruitfulness.
47. A Life of Length and Happiness.
48. The Judge, a Court of Justice, Judgment.
49. Greed, Love of Money.
50. Relief, Forgiveness, Freedom.

60. Loss of the Husband or Wife.
70. Science, Virtues, Graces, Initiation.
75. Lust, The World and the Flesh.
77. Forgiveness, Contrition, Penitence.
80. Protection, Recovery from Sickness or Accident.
81. The Adept.
90. Affliction, Grief, Mistakes, Blindness.
100. God's Favour, the Angels and High Spirits.
120. Honour, Love of Country, Praise.
200. Uncertainty, Hesitancy, Fear.
215. Grief, Misfortune.
300. Protection, True Belief, Philosophy.
318. God's Messenger.
350. Justice, Hope.
360. Society, Home, a House.
365. Astrology and Astronomy.
400. Long Travels.
490. Priestly Lore, Ministers of Religion Generally.
500. Virtue, Sanctity.
600. The Number of Perfection.
666. Enmity, Secret Plots, Maliciousness.
700. Power, Might.
800. Conquest, Empire.
900. Struggles, Eruptions, Inharmony, War.
1000. The Number of Sympathy and Mercy.
1095. Silence, Reserve.
1260. Worries, Terrors.
1390. Persecution.

An example will suffice to show how this Quaballah is usually applied and understood. Take again the names Napoleon Buonaparte and Bonaparte.

	1			**2**			**3**	
N	equals	40	B	equals	2	B	equals	2
A	„	1	U	„	200	O	„	50
P	„	60	O	„	50	N	„	40
O	„	50	N	„	40	A	„	1
L	„	20	A	„	1	P	„	60
E	„	5	P	„	60	A	„	1
O	„	50	A	„	1	R	„	80
N	„	40	R	„	80	T	„	100
		—	T	„	100	E	„	5
		266	E	„	5			—
					—			339
					539			

Now add No. 1 and No. 2 together, equals $\begin{cases} 539 \\ 266 \end{cases}$

$$\overline{}$$
$$805$$

The names Napoleon Buonaparte are contained in 805, which is—

equals 800, Conquest, Empire.

      5, Marriage, Pleasure, Happiness, The Stars.

Now add No. 1 and No. 3 together, equals $\begin{cases} 266 \\ 339 \end{cases}$

$$\overline{}$$
$$605$$

The names Napoleon Bonaparte are contained in 605, which is—

      600, the Number of Perfection.

      5, Marriage, etc.

This is partially correct with regard to Napoleon, " The Stars " being the symbols of destiny.

Let us take another example—John Milton.

J equals	600		M equals	30
O ,,	50		I ,,	9
H ,,	8		L ,,	20
N ,,	40		T ,,	100
	698		O ,,	50
			N ,,	40
				249

The names John Milton are contained in (249 plus 698) 947—

equals 900, Struggles, Eruptions, Inharmony.

47, Life of Length and Happiness.

Partially correct.

As a final example, we will take the names William Makepeace Thackeray—

W equals	1400		M equals	30		T equals	100
I ,,	9		A ,,	1		H ,,	8
L ,,	20		K ,,	10		A ,,	1
L ,,	20		E ,,	5		C ,,	3
I ,,	9		P ,,	60		K ,,	10
A ,,	1		E ,,	5		E ,,	5
M ,,	30		A ,,	1		R ,,	80
	1489		C ,,	3		A ,,	1
			E ,,	5		Y ,,	400
				120			608

Now collect the powers and add them together :—

William	.	.	.	1489
Makepeace	.	.	.	120
Thackeray	.	.	.	608
				2217

It will be seen that this number exceeds the greatest limit, which is 1390. In cases of this kind it is only needful to cut off the first number and obtain an interpretation from the remaining figures. Therefore, on removing the two in the number 2217, we have left 217—

equals 200, Uncertainty, Hesitancy, Fear.
17, Misfortune, Carelessness.

Not very correct.

It will be seen that this method of dealing with the values given is not the correct way. Pythagoras taught of the " music of the Spheres," and it is probable that in accepting the letter values we should consider the *sound* only of the word to be dealt with and not the number of letters contained in it, as in the Hebrew Quaballah. Thus JOHN is simply JON, and must be so regarded. It seems that there are flaws in this Pythagorean system which the student will discover for himself and will perchance be able to rectify ; for in this branch of study untiring energy is an essential, and without it no deep success is gained. The great Boëthius, called " the last of the Romans," has preserved the Pythagorean numerals for us. They were formed as follows :—

The Greek letters and their corresponding numerals are correctly—

Alpha 1	Iota 10	Rho 100
Beta 2	Kappa 20	Sigma 200
Gamma 3	Lambda 30	Tau 300
Delta 4	Mu 40	Upsilon 400
Epsilon 5	Nu 50	Phi 500
Episemon 6	Xi 60	Chi 600
Zeta 7	Omicron 70	Psi 700
Eta 8	Pi 80	Omega 800
Theta 9	Koppa 90	Sanpi 900
	Alpha (with dash) 1000	

Mr Willis Whitehead has constructed a Quaballah from the Greek, which he calls "the most simple and natural, its 24 symbols corresponding with the hours of the day and the houses of the Zodiac." I cannot write as to its employment, but as it may be of interest I give it here:—

Alpha (A) equals 1.

Beta (B) equals 2.

Gamma (G) equals 3.

Delta (D) equals 4.

Epsilon (E W V) equals 5.

Zeta (Z) equals 6.

Eta (E long) equals 7.

Theta (H Th) equals 8.

Iota (J I Y) equals 9.

Kappa (K) equals 10.

Lambda (L) equals 11.

Mu (M) equals 12.

Nu (N) equals 13.

Xi (X S) equals 14.

Omicron (O short) equals 15.

Pi (P) equals 16.

Rho (R) equals 17.

Sigma (S) equals 18.

Tau (T) equals 19.

Upsilon (U) equals 20.

Phi (F P H) equals 21.

Chi (C CH) equals 22.

Psi (P S) equals 23.

Omega (O long) equals 24.

In the next chapter another system of divination by numbers ascribed to Pythagoras will be explained.

CHAPTER IV

HOW TO PROPHESY BY NUMBERS

(Ascribed to Pythagoras)

In this Quaballah the letters are numbered as follows :—

2 Y	11 I J N	21 G
3 Z	12 E L R P	26 C
4 A F S	13 X	28 H
6 B T	16 K	
8 Q	18 D W	
9 O U V	19 M	

The Planets as follows :—

Moon 45	Mars 39
Mercury 114	Jupiter 78
Venus 45	Saturn 55
Sun 34	

And also the days of the week :—

Sunday 106	Thursday 31
Monday 52	Friday 68
Tuesday 52	Saturday 45
Wednesday 102	

The magic square to be used in connection with the letters, days, and planets is divided into four compartments, and includes the numbers from 1 to 30, arranged as follows :—

Section I. contains the numbers 1, 2, 3, 4, 7, 9, 11, 13, 14.

Section II. contains the numbers 10, 16, 17, 18, 20, 21, 24, 26, 27.

Section III. contains the numbers 5, 6, 8, 12, 15, 19, 23.

Section IV. contains the numbers 22, 25, 28, 29, 30.

Section I. indicates success in a little time.

Section II. indicates success after some worry or delay.

Section III. indicates speedy failure.

Section IV. indicates failure after the lapse of time.

Section I. is springtime and youth.

Section II. is autumn and tall dark people.

Section III. is summer and short fair people.

Section IV. is winter and short dark people.

To make use of the foregoing information, the first thing to be done is to think of a number; any number from 1 to 30 can be employed. This will be found more satisfactory than using higher numbers. Add to this the numerical value of the initial letter of your Christian name; again add to this the value of the day of the week on which you seek the information; add to this again the value of the planet " ruling " (astrologically speaking) the day.

Moon rules Monday.   Mars rules Tuesday.
Mercury rules Wednesday. Jupiter rules Thursday.
Venus rules Friday.   Saturn rules Saturday.
Sun rules Sunday.

Divide the result thus obtained by 30, and the remainder indicates the answer according to the section of the square it may happen to be in. As an example I select : What will be the future of the modern great ironclads ? *First* number thought of 28—day Thursday—then we proceed as follows :—

Number *first* thought of . . .	28
+ Initial of Christian name (Isidore) = I .	11
+ Number for Thursday	31
+ Jupiter's Number	78
	148

Divide 148 by 30 ; this gives us 4 and 28 over—28 is the indicator. It is found in the fourth section of the magic square, and is an answer which, of course, can easily be assumed ; but the idea is meant to guide us in some way with regard to important questions concerning ourselves. The old masters retired from the mass of men, and after offering their heartfelt prayers to God, implored for light. The soul of man is, by virtue of its Divine origin, all-knowing, but error arises from the grossness with which it is surrounded, and which it is required to refine and purify. Hence frivolous questions are an insult to the higher part of man and should be avoided. All spiritual philosophy seeks for the betterment of man and for his spiritual redemption, and all spiritual affairs demand a serious and dignified attitude. This simple system is ascribed to Pythagoras and may be authentic. In 1657 Sieur de Peruchio published a work in Paris, dealing comprehensively with this subject. One question

only demands a slight variation in method, and that
is in cases of sickness, when the moon's age must be
added before division can be made.   The first day
of the moon is at new moon, the second the day
following, etc., until the next new moon.   For
example, William asks : Will my sick wife recover ?

Number thought of	3
+ Initial of Christian name (William) = W.	18
+ Number for Thursday	31
+ Jupiter's number	78
+ Moon's age	22
	—
	152

Divide 152 by 30 ; this gives us 5 and 2 over—2
is the indicator.   It is found in the first section of
the magic square.   The following days in each
month are considered evil for employing this method
of divination—

January, 3, 4, 5, 9, 11.	July, 16, 19.
February, 7, 13, 17, 19.	August, 8, 16.
March, 13, 15, 16.	September, 1, 15, 16.
April, 5, 14	October, 16.
May, 8, 14.	November, 15, 16.
June, 6.	December, 6, 7, 11.

In conclusion, I may add that if after division is
made there is no remainder, then the number 30
must be accepted as indicator.[1]

[1] This method of divination is given in detail in *A Manual of
Cartomancy*, by Grand Orient.   Publishers, William Rider & Son,
Ltd., London.   2s. 6d. net

CHAPTER V

ARITHMETICAL DIVINATION

By an ingenious and entirely Quaballistic management of dates, G. P. Philomeste, A.B., and other French occult writers have produced some remarkable results, mention of which can hardly be omitted in a work of this kind. For example, 1789 is the year of the destruction of the Bastille and the beginning of the great French Revolution. Then 1789 added together thus, 1 plus 7 plus 8 plus 9 equals 25, and 25 added to 1789 is (1789 plus 25 equals 1814) 1814, the year Napoleon left Fontainebleau for Elba. The ill-fated Louis XVI. succeeded to the throne in the year 1774, equals 1 plus 7 plus 7 plus 4 equals 19, and 19 added to 1774 is (1774 plus 19 equals 1793) 1793, the year of his and his queen's (Marie Antoinette) death by public execution. In 1853 Louis Napoleon was married (27 days after he was declared Emperor) to the Countess of Montijo at Notre Dame. 1853 equals 1 plus 8 plus 5 plus 3 equals 17, and if we add 17 to 1853 we get 1870, the year of the Franco-Prussian war and the downfall of the Emperor. Again, the last Napoleon was married and proclaimed Emperor of the French in the year 1853:

he was born in the year 1808, equals 1 plus 8 plus
0 plus 8 equals 17, and by adding this 17 to 1853
we also get the year of his overthrow. The Empress was born in the year 1826, equals 1 plus 8
plus 2 plus 6 equals also 17, which, added to the
year of her marriage, 1853, brings us again to
1870. From a book by Peignot, Mr W. Jones,
F.S.A., derives the following curious information :—

Louis IX. was born in 1215, equals 1 plus 2 plus 1
plus 5 equals 9, his titular number ; Charles VII.
was born in 1402, equals 1 plus 4 plus 0 plus 2
equals 7 ; Louis XII. was born in 1461, equals 1 plus
4 plus 6 plus 1 equals 12 ; Louis XVIII. was born
in 1755, equals 1 plus 7 plus 5 plus 5 equals 18.

In the year 1848 the then Prussian Crown Prince
consulted an occult student in Berlin, and was
told that he would ascend the throne in the year
1849. The scholar then added the number 1, 8,
4, 9 together, and obtaining thereby the number
22, he added it to 1849, thus—

$$1849$$
$$22$$
$$\overline{}$$
$$1871$$

In this year the King of Prussia became Emperor of Germany. The numbers 1, 8, 7, 1 were
again added, and the result 17 was added to 1871,
thus—

$$1871$$
$$17$$
$$\overline{}$$
$$1888$$

In the year 1888 the Prince was told there would be 3 Emperors. Then he added the number 1888 together and obtained 25. This result was added to 1888, thus—

$$1888$$
$$25$$

$$1913$$

and in the year 1913 a terrible war was predicted. Astrologers have observed with much concern the approaching unfavourable indications, which will not clear off for some time after the year 1913. It remains to be seen now if great nations are far enough advanced to turn the power of Mars from war, murder, and destruction (its lower and degraded side) into energy and activity (its higher side). At the present day war would be no glory; victory no benefit, and no honour; and woe be unto the striker of the first blow. The misery and terror of a modern war can hardly be conceived, nor can its horror be in any way over-estimated. The whole medical skill of the world will not be enough to " patch up " the wearied and shattered bodies of brave men. Brave women at home will cry out for the father and the son, and their deep curses will rise to heaven; and they of the nations who by their clumsiness have brought on such terrible disaster will be torn to pieces by a tormented people. Spiritual people all the world over, from the throne to the cabin, will pray that the growing civilisation of nations be not checked and thrown back by so horrible a disease as war, and the monarchs and rulers of the world and their ministers will be loved, blessed, and glory crowned, if by Divine grace, in their earthly power, they refuse to permit this crime against mankind, and with the powerful words, " Love thy neighbour as thy self," before their eyes, they make it impossible that any misunderstanding between nations should be decided by so crude a method as that of the sword.

CHAPTER VI

GOOD AND EVIL DAYS

THE ancient philosophers were wont to judge days of good or evil import by applying the following rules :—

TO DISCOVER LUCKY DAYS

(*a*) Note the day of full moon. (This can easily be found in almost any almanac.)

(*b*) Count the number of days from that day until the end of the month.

(*c*) Multiply the number of days the month contains by the number of days from full moon until the end of the month, and the result will be your answer.

Example.—Full moon at Melbourne fell on April 19th in the year 1905. There are 30 days in April, and from the 19th until the 30th there are just 11 days. Multiply the number of days contained in the entire month, viz. 30, by the number of days from full moon to the end of the month, viz. 11—equals 30 multiplied by 11 equals 330.

The fortunate days in April 1905 are thus shown to be the 3rd and the 30th.

If the result, instead of 330, had been 303, the answer would be the same. Had the result been 414, the days would have been the 4th and the 14th, and if it had been 441, it would have been the same. Again, had it been 544, the days would have been the 5th and the 4th, the 4th becoming exceptionally strong by repetition.

To Find the Unlucky Days

(*a*) Find as before the date of full moon.

(*b*) Count the number of days before full moon.

(*c*) Multiply the number of days before full moon by the number of days the month contains.

Full moon fell on the 19th of the month. We therefore multiply the number of days in the month by the number of days preceding full moon, viz. 18—equals 30 multiplied by 18 equals 540.

Now it is evident that we cannot employ the cipher, therefore we must eliminate it altogether, and account the 5th and 4th unlucky days in April 1905.

NOTE.—Should it so happen that a date indicated as fortunate falls also amongst the unfortunate indications, then that date must be accounted unfortunate, it being an old belief that in most mundane matters the evil was more powerful than the good.

Lucky Marriage Days

A betrothed lady wishes to know which days are the most fortunate for her marriage. She would ascertain this by employing the following rules :—

(*a*) Find the day of full moon.

(*b*) Note the number of days in the month.

(*c*) Find the number of days from full moon to the end of the month.

(*d*) Deduct the number of days from the full of the moon to the end of the month from the number of days in the month, and multiply remainder by her age.

Example.—The lady is 24 years of age, and wishes to find her fortunate marriage days in December—

Full moon equals December 12th.

Number of days in month equals 31.

Number of days from full moon to the end of month equals 19.

Deduct 19 from 31 equals 12.

Lady's age equals 24.

Then 24 multiplied by 12 equals 288.

Therefore the lucky days are the 28th and the 8th of December 1905. This must be proved by considering the unlucky days—

Date of full moon, December 12th.

Number of days in the month equals 31.

Number of days preceding full moon equals 11.

Lady's age equals 24.

Multiply the number of days preceding full moon by the lady's age—equals 11 multiplied by 24 equals 264 (26, 4), therefore the 26th and 4th are evil days for the event, and as these two dates are different from the dates found as lucky, the fortunate days are proved to be the 8th and the 28th of the month.

NOTE.—Reference should also be made to the

planetary positions and aspects on these days before making final selection. The "harmony of the Heavens" was considered as wisdom and demanded that—"To everything there is a season and a *time* for every purpose ; a time to be born, a time to die ; a time to plant, and a time to pluck up that which is planted ; a time to get, and a time to lose ; a time of war, and a time of peace" (Eccles. iii. 1, 2, 6–8).

As regards the age of a person, it may be remarked that after a lapse of six months from the last birthday, the age for the coming birthday is the right one to take. For example, a lady is 23 years and 6 months. She would be considered as 24 for calculating purposes ; but if she is but 23 and, say, 3 months, then 23 should be employed.

CHAPTER VII

GOOD AND EVIL DAYS—*continued*

THE following extract from an old MS. has been utilised by several writers on occult subjects. I give it in its ancient dress for the sake of its quaintness :—

" We read of an old Arabian philosopher, a man of divers rare observations, who did remark three Mundayes in a year to be most unfortunate to begin any notable work, viz. ye first Munday of April, ye wch day Cain was borne and his brother Abell slaine. Ye 2nd is ye first Munday of August, ye wch day Sodom and Gomorrah were confounded. Ye 3rd is ye last Munday of December, ye wch day Judas Iscariott was borne. These three dayes, together with ye Innocents' Day, by divers of the learned are reputed to be most unfortunate of all dayes, and ought to be eschewed by all men for ye great mishaps wch often do occur in them." (On the first Monday in August 1895, the massacre of missionaries in China took place.) " And thus much concerning ye opinion of our Ancient of dayes. So in like manner I will repeat unto you yt be observed by some old writers, chiefly ye ancient astrologians who did allege that there were 28 dayes in ye yeare wch were revealed by the Angell Gabriel to ye Good Joseph wch ever have been remarked to be very fortunate dayes to cure wounds, sow seeds, plant trees, build houses or take journies, in fighting or giving of battaill. They also doe alledge that children who were borne in any of these dayse could never be poore ; and all children who were put to schooles or colledges in those dayes should become great schollars, and those who were put to any craft or trade in such dayes should become perfect artificers and rich, and such as were put to trade in marchandise should become most wealthy. Ye dayes be these—ye 3rd and 13th of January ; ye 5th and 28th of February ; ye 3rd, 22nd, and 30th of March ; ye 5th, 22nd, and 29th of April ; ye 4th and 28th of May ; ye 3rd and 8th of June ; ye 12th, 18th, and 15th of July ; ye 12th of August ; ye 1st, 7th, 24th, and 28th of September ; ye 4th and 15th of October ; ye 13th and 19th of November ; ye 23rd and 26th of December."

In the Cottonian Manuscripts, the three Dies Mali (Days of Evil) of the year are set down as the last Monday in April ; " and then is the second at the coming in (*i.e.* the first half of the month) of the month we call August ; then is the third, which is the first Monday of the going out (*i.e.* the last half of the month) of the month of December."

In an old book (*Book of Presidents*—precedents), published in London in 1616, the following days are those " the Egyptians note to be dangerous to begin or take anything in hand, as to take a journey or any such like thing " :—

January 1, 2, 4, 5, 10, 15, 17, 19.
February 7, 10, 17, 27, 28.
March 15, 16, 28.

April 7, 10, 16, 20, 21.
May 7, 15, 20.
June 4, 10, 22.

July 15, 20.
August 1, 19, 20, 29, 30.
September 3, 4, 6, 7, 21, 22.
October 4, 16, 24.
November 5, 6, 28, 29.
December 6, 7, 9, 15, 17, 22.

Long before the foregoing list was published in the *Book of Presidents*, the following 32 evil days were noted in a MS. of the early 15th century :—

January 1, 2, 4, 5, 7, 10, 15.
February 6, 7, 18.
March 1, 6, 8.
April 6, 11.
May 5, 6, 7.
June 7, 15.

July 5, 19.
August 15, 19.
September 6, 7.
October 6.
November 15, 16.
December 15, 16, 17.

The faith of the writer of this MS. in that Great Power which guides the planets and rules the universe is expressed in the line—" Sed tamen in Domino confido " (Nevertheless I will trust in the Lord).

Another list of unlucky days for men, of old much regarded, is—

January 3, 4.

February 6, 7, 12, 13, 19, 20.
March 5, 6, 12, 13.

May 12, 13, 20, 21, 26, 27.

June 1, 2, 9, 10, 16, 17, 22, 23, 24.
July 3, 4, 10, 11, 16, 17, 18.
October 3, 4, 9, 10, 11, 16, 17, 31.
November 1, 3.

And those which women are warned to avoid and bear themselves cautiously in connection with are—

January 5, 6, 13, 14, 20, 21.	July 3, 4.
February 2, 3, 9, 10, 16, 17, 22, 23.	September 9, 16.
March 1, 2, 8, 9, 16, 17, 28, 29.	October 20, 27.
April 24, 25.	November 9, 10, 21, 29, 30.
May 1, 2, 9, 17, 22, 29, 30.	December 6, 14, 21.
June 5, 6, 12, 13, 18, 19.	

Those considered fortunate for love matters are :—

January 1, 2, 15, 26, 27, 28.	July 9, 14, 15, 20.
February 11, 21, 25, 26.	August 6, 7, 10, 11, 16, 20, 25.
March 10, 24.	September 4, 8, 17, 18, 23.
April 6, 15, 16, 20, 28.	October 3, 7, 16, 21, 22.
May 3, 13, 18, 31.	November 5, 14, 20.
June 10, 11, 15, 22, 25.	December 15, 19, 20, 22, 23, 25.

The virtues of these old lists I have never had opportunity to consider, and it is possible that each person has some days of good and some days of ill luck during the year ; for example, the 3rd of September is set down as evil in the *Book of Presidents*, yet for Oliver Cromwell it was most fortunate, and the Protector always considered it so. It was an evil day for the town of Northampton, which was destroyed by fire, September 3rd, 1675. Again, the 3rd of November was considered of ill omen for men, yet it was equally unfortunate for women in the year 1069, for on that date, according to Stow, the famous antiquary and annalist, the sea broke over the land in England and Scotland, causing terrible destruction ; and as history always repeats itself, it was the date of the great storm in 1703. Amongst my records I have an account of a man who every 26th of August had an accident of a more or less serious nature, and this, and many other similar incidents easy to be produced, places the matter beyond that which we are too fond of contemptuously relegating to chance.

CHAPTER VIII

OTHER QUABALLAHS

I

THE ARABIC

THE Arabic alphabet consists of 28 letters varying in shape according to their position at the beginning, middle, or end of words. The letters have special numerical values, by the aid of which the Arabs are able to do many wonderful things. It must not be forgotten that the Arabic is a phonetic language and beautifully adapted for purposes of prophecy. At the side of each Arabic sound I am giving the English equivalent and numerical value :—

Alif	(A)	equals	1	Zine	(Z)	equals	7
Ba	(B)	,,	2	Seen	(S)	,,	60
Ta	(T)	,,	400	Sheen	(Sh)	,,	300
Sa	(S)	,,	500	Sad	(S)	,,	90
Jeem	(J)	,,	3	Dad	(D)	,,	800
Ha	(H)	,,	8	Ta	(T)	,,	9
Kha	(Kh)	,,	600	Za	(Z)	,,	900
Dal	(D)	,,	4	Aine	(A)	,,	70
Zal	(Z)	,,	700	Ghine	(Gh)	,,	1000
Ra	(R)	,,	200	Fa	(F)	,,	80

Kaf	(K) equals 100	Noon	(N)	equals	50
Kaf	(K) „ 20	Waw (U W O) „			6
Lam	(L) „ 30	Ha	(H)	„	5
Meem (M)	„ 40	Ya	(Y)	„	10

In adapting this Quaballah to our own language, some difficulties present themselves, on account of a letter like H, for instance, having two values, viz. 8 and 5, but the 8 is a hard throat sound, rarely met with in English, to which language the 5 is more adaptable, and so it is with A, D, K, T, S, and Z. The same difficulty with the letter H is met with in adapting the Hebrew Quaballah to English use. I have accepted H as of value 5, excepting under special circumstances. For practical use the Arabic Quaballah can be further reduced so as to embrace all English letters and sounds.

II

An English Quaballah used in the transmitting of secret messages was sent to me by Mr H. Burston. It may interest the student from curiosity, if not in a practical way:—

A	85	H	64	O	80	V	12
B	16	I	80	P	17	W	20
C	30	J	4	Q	5	X	4
D	44	K	8	R	62	Y	20
E	120	L	40	S	80	Z	2
F	25	M	30	T	90		
G	17	N	80	U	34		

There are several others of this kind, but the above example is sufficient for the present.

III

A MODERN QUABALLAH

The following extracts from the *Sunday Times*, Sydney, June 14th, 1903, sent me by Mr J. Nicholas, will be found interesting, as illustrating a new system of numeration, introduced by a lady teacher of music in the United States, " who makes a specialty of teaching musical composition. In studying vibrations and harmony, somewhat beyond the point that has as yet been set down in books, she thinks she has found that each digit and each letter has a uniform vibration. She says, as a matter of fact, that there is no such thing as chance ; that everything is relevant, and signifies, and that a rose by any other name, however sweet it might be, would not be a rose, since a name is of importance.

"The alphabet, digit, and law of vibration are the foundation of the system. It is declared that the alphabet of every language is of deep import, and is not only in itself prophetic, but interprets prophecy, as it relates to the people who use it.

"The system divides the alphabet into three divisions or degrees. The first nine letters constitute the first degree, the next nine the second degree, and the last eight the third degree.

"Each letter is represented by a digit number, as follows :—A, J, and S are represented by 1 in

each of the three degrees ; B, K, and T, by 2 ;
C, L, and U, by 3 ; D, M, and V, by 4 ; E, N, and
W, by 5 ; F, O, and X, by 6 ; Y, P, and G, by 7 ;
H, Q, and Z, by 8 ; and I and R, by 9, there being
no ninth letter in the third degree.

SIGNIFICANCE OF FIGURES

" The significance of each number and letter of
the first degree is as follows :—One is the beginning,
the father; 2, the mother, or moulder; 3, the
created ; 4, the matter, the physical ; 5, the
duality of man ; 6, the pattern of all building ;
7, the completed temple ; 8, the manifestation of
God ; 9, revelation. The other two degrees, with
some slight differences, are simply an intensifica-
tion of the first.

" As an illustration, take the name and birth
dates of the late Pope Leo XIII. The letters of his
name, Joachim, are represented by the following
numbers :—1, 6, 1, 3, 8, 9, 4. Add these, and the
sum is 32. Add again, as all numbers are reduced
to a digit, and the sum is 5. In the last name,
Pecci, the letters represent 7, 5, 3, 3, 9. The sum
of these numbers is 27. Adding again to get the
digit, we have 9. March is the third month, and
the late Pope was born the second day of that
month, 1810. Adding the numbers of the year,
we have 10. This makes the numbers from
which the concord is determined 5 and 9, which
represent the name, and 3, 2, 10 the birth.

" Ten, being 1 intensified, the numbers of the
late Pope's birth represent the first three great

principles.   Ten is said to represent a person who is sufficient unto himself, and this is especially true if a factor of 10 is found in the name, as the 5 in this case.   According to this system, these numbers form a combination which indicates, in part at least, the strong and remarkable character of the man.''

CHAPTER IX

COLOURS, METALS, AND GEMS IN HARMONY WITH THE NUMBERS

I ALLOT the following colours, metals, and gems to the numbers. Units are taken from 1 to 9; after 9 the series begins again, as, for example, 10 equals 1, 11 equals 2, 12 equals 3, etc. :—

Numbers.	Colours.	Metals.	Stones.
1	Yellow, Orange, Gold.	Gold.	Diamond, Ruby.
2	Glistening White, Silvery colours, Light Greens, Pearly tints.	Silver.	Moonstone, Onyx.
3	Purple, Azure.	Tin.	Turquoise, Carbuncle.
4	Yellow, Orange, Gold.	Gold.	Diamond, Ruby.
5	Light Blue, Blue Slate colour, Light Grey.	Quicksilver.	Hyacinth.

Numbers.	Colours.	Metals.	Stones.
6	Green, Art shades, Crimson, Pale Blue.	Copper.	Emerald, Opal.
7	Glistening White, Silvery colours, Light Greens, Pearly tints.	Silver.	Moonstone, Onyx.
8	Black, Dark Brown, Dark Blue.	Lead.	Onyx, Lapis Lazuli.
9	Red, Scarlet.	Iron.	Amethyst, Topaz.

CHAPTER X

CONCLUSION

In the foregoing pages I have given a brief outline of a subject, which, if submitted to a more technical and intricate treatment, would fill several volumes with ease. My desire to present the matter in an elementary style will, I hope, prove useful to students, and carry out for general readers my desire to interest, instruct, and to amuse. Beside the scholars in this special knowledge mentioned in these pages, I must not forget the name of Mr David Cope, a learned master, with whom I have spent many pleasant hours investigating problems in occult mathematics. John Heydon, author of the *Holy Guide*, now so very hard to obtain, was one of the best known Rosicrucian apologists of 17th-century England. He studied at Oxford, and joined King Charles's forces in the Civil War, obtaining the command of a troop of horse. " I never violated any man," he says, " nor defaced the memory of saint or martyr. I never killed a man wilfully, but took him prisoner, and disarmed him. I did never divide myself from any man upon the difference of opinion, or was angry with his judgment. I never regarded what religion any man was," etc. His published works number about eleven. Eliphas Levi, the great French Quaballist, was the son of a poor Paris shoemaker. His birth name was Alphonse Louis Constant, and he was born about the year 1809. He was a fine Hebrew scholar, and translated into the French language some remarkable works. He passed from earth in the year 1875. Throughout this treatise I have used the spelling Quaballah in preference to the better known Kabala and Cabala.

Regarding the Quaballahs, I personally prefer the Hebrew, to which the first and second chapters of this book are devoted. I think that the examples I produce will justify my recast of the values of the letters. I trust that this book will serve a useful purpose, and combine with the works of others who are striving to throw a little more light on the many dark caverns wholly unexplored by modern materialistic science.